REAL TO REEL

Reading and Listening

Samuela Eckstut
Despina Scoulos

NEWBURY HOUSE PUBLISHERS, Cambridge
A division of Harper & Row, Publishers, Inc.
New York, Philadelphia, San Francisco, Washington
London, Mexico City, São Paulo, Singapore, Sydney
1986

Library of Congress Cataloging-in-Publication Data

Ekstut, Samuela.
    Real to reel.

    2. English language--Text-books for foreign
speakers.   I. Scoulos, Despina.   II. Title.
PE1128.E344   1986   428.3'4   85-21734
ISBN 0-88377-316-3

Cover and Interior Design by Carson Designs
Illustrations by Kathy Kelleher

NEWBURY HOUSE PUBLISHERS
A division of Harper & Row, Publishers, Inc.

Language Science
Language Teaching
Language Learning

CAMBRIDGE, MASSACHUSETTS

First printing: March 1986
2   6 8 10 9 7 5

Printed in the U.S.A.

The authors would like to thank Karen Sorensen and Sheila and Tony Lambie for their advice and suggestions.

Credits

The authors wish to thank the following organizations for permission to reproduce material appearing on the pages indicated:

Contents

ROUND THREE

TO THE TEACHER

Overview

Real to Reel is for elementary/low-intermediate students of ESL/EFL both in the United States and abroad. The emphasis of the course is on doing things in English rather than simply learning about it. The majority of activities simulate what students might actually read, write, listen to, or say in natural contexts.

The book consists of 27 units divided into three "rounds" of nine units each. Each unit should take from 2 to 4 hours to complete depending on the amount of extra work the teacher does and whether the students do the writing tasks at home or in class.

Organization

Each unit has a general theme and is organized according to skills. The themes appear three times in the book, once in each round. For example, At Work appears in Units Four (Round 1), Thirteen (Round 2), and Twenty-two (Round 3). Students go around the themes three times, doing Round 1 before Round 2, and Round 2 before Round 3. Each round recycles structures and functions and introduces students to more complex language and progressively more difficult tasks.

Authentic material

The reading texts are authentic and expose students to the type of English they will deal with in nonclassroom situations. Although the texts contain vocabulary and structures which students have not met before, the tasks they are asked to do are within their active ability.

The language in the taped material contains simulated authentic language recorded at normal speed with all the hesitations, repetitions, and redundancies of natural speech. Again, although students will not recognize every vocabulary item or grammatical structure, the focused tasks are within the students' level of ability. The activities give attention to specific areas rather than demand that students understand the whole, which is often frustrating to them.

Through constant exposure to authentic written and spoken English, students learn strategies to handle language that is above their linguistic ability, thereby building their confidence and bridging the gap between real and classroom English.

Reading

Description

Each unit begins with the reading text and one or two prereading activities. These activities familiarize students with the subject of the text, practice skills such as scanning, skimming, and predicting, and give students a reason for reading the text.

The exercises that follow the texts teach comprehension rather than test it. They help students understand a text which they may initially have found difficult. They also practice skills which students can transfer to reading outside the classroom. These skills include:

guessing meaning from context
recognizing and understanding cohesive devices
interpreting discourse markers
extracting details
identifying the main idea

The exercises focus students' attention on parts of the text as opposed to the whole and show them that even if a text has many unknown words, they can understand select information in it. The exercises also reflect the fact that people read different types of texts for different reasons. In Unit Eight students scan several tables of contents to locate page numbers and subject matter, but in Unit Twenty-six they read a text on drowning to extract details.

Suggestions for use

Ask students warm-up questions to preteach vocabulary and to get them to predict the contents of the text by using their existing knowledge of the subject. This is a strategy good readers use but which students do not often transfer to English language learning.

Preteach the words and phrases which students will need to complete the comprehension exercises. Design the warm-up questions in such a way that you can elicit some of the vocabulary from the class. Examples of such questions are:

(Unit Eighteen) When's your birthday? What's your horoscope sign? Do you read horoscopes? Do you believe what horoscopes say?

(Unit Nineteen) Have your heard of Disneyland? Where is it? What is it? Who was Walt Disney? Why is he famous?

(Unit Twenty-six) How can swimming be dangerous? What do you do if someone is drowning? What can you throw into the water to save a drowning person? What should you do when the drowning person is out of the water?

Have the students read the text initially to find the answers to the prereading exercises. Go over the answers and then ask students to read the text again and do the comprehension exercises. Make sure students justify their answers by referring to the appropriate sections of the text.

Listening

Description

The listening activities include conversations, news broadcasts, recorded messages, announcements, and lectures, all of which are natural extensions of the unit themes. The tasks reflect what people might do when they listen to such discourse. The type of tasks students have to do include taking notes, filling in forms and charts, and making guesses.

Through constant exposure to a natural stretch of spoken English, students learn to "tune their ear." As they go through the course, they gain more and more familiarity with real spoken English and feel more comfortable listening to it outside the classroom.

Suggestions for use

Before class check the tapescript for new vocabulary items which students will need to know to complete the task. Preteach this vocabulary and go over the pronunciation. Ask students to read the directions and accompanying material. Where appropriate, ask students to predict the answers and then check their predictions against the tape. An example of this is the itinerary on page 178. Go over any unknown vocabulary and check that students understand what they are to do.

As a general rule, play the tape through once without stopping. At the second listening, stop the tape at intervals to give students time to write.

Go over the answers with the entire class or ask students to compare answers in pairs. As a final activity, play the tape through again without stopping in order to have the students listen to the discourse as a connected whole.

Speaking

Description

The speaking activities get students to communicate with each other using the range of structures usually taught at the elementary level. The variety of speaking activities maintains students' interest and provides a representative sample of the type of communicative activities students may engage in outside the classroom. These activities require students to express functions such as:

> describing people, places, and objects
> asking about and giving personal information
> making, accepting, and refusing suggestions
> giving instructions
> making comparisons
> narrating

Students carry out these functions through a variety of information exchanges, role plays, discussions, and games.

Many speaking activities include a Useful Language section. This section provides students with model language and gives them the support they need to do the task with confidence. As they progress through the course, students should become less and less dependent on the Useful Language sections. In fact, teachers may choose to ignore them in the later units.

Suggestions for use

These are general guidelines, which will vary depending upon the activity:

Ask students to read the directions. Preteach essential vocabulary. Where pictures are provided, ask students to describe them.

Draw students' attention to the Useful Language section. Go over the structures involved and practice the pronunciation using choral repetition where necessary. A further suggestion is to elicit other ways of expressing the same functions. For example, ask students what language they would use for the activity. Put their ideas on the board and/or ask them to compare their suggestions with those in the Useful Language section.

Set an example. When there are two roles, take the role of Student A and ask a student to take the role of Student B. Then switch roles. Finally, ask two students to do the activity in front of the class and then to switch roles and do it again.

Divide the class into pairs or groups. For activities that involve information exchanges or role plays, divide each pair into Student A and Student B. Student A should look only at Student A's material and Student B at Student B's material. For these kinds of exercises, Student A will find his or her material in the main text, while Student B will find another set of material as indicated at the back of the book.

Ask the students to do the activity. In role plays students should switch roles when they have finished the first time so that they get the chance to do both roles.

Walk around the class and monitor the activity. As a general rule, do not correct students at this stage, as it may discourage them and break the flow of the activity. Deal with serious group errors in a remedial lesson and individual problems during breaks or after class.

When the students come together after a discussion, have them report their findings or ideas to the class as a whole.

For group work, appoint a group secretary when you first divide the class into groups. This person will take notes and report back at the end of the discussion. Alternatively, tell all the students to take notes and choose a spokesperson at the end. This encoruages everyone to listen carefully during the activity. A third suggestion is to redivide the groups at the end of the activity. For example, if the students are in groups of four, they change groups like this:

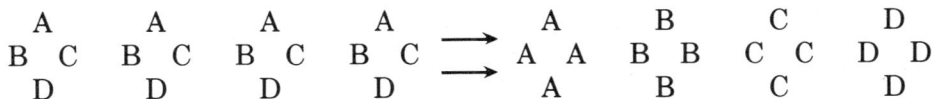

```
   A        A        A        A    ⟶    A     B     C     D
 B   C    B   C    B   C    B   C   ⟶   A  A  B  B  C  C  D  D
   D        D        D        D          A     B     C     D
```

Students then report the discussion of their previous group to their new group.

Writing

Description

The writing activities include describing objects, people, and places, requesting information, and writing directions and instructions. They help students consolidate language they have practiced orally and develop skills such as sequencing ideas, connecting sentences, using cohesive devices, and writing coherent paragraphs. The tasks are connected to previous activities and/or the theme of the unit. They are designed to reflect some of the writing activities that people actually do and stress working through a text as a connected whole as opposed to writing sentences in isolation.

Suggestions for use

Students can do the writing tasks in class or at home. Ask them to read the model text and check that they have understood it by asking check questions such as the following for the writing activity on page 26:

Who is the message to?
Who is the message from?
Who called?
What time did she call?
Who can't meet her?
Where are they going?
When do they want to meet her?

Point out particular features such as format and punctuation, and answer questions about vocabulary.

Ask students to make notes before they do the assignment. In this way you can give them vocabulary they need and encourage them to jot down their ideas before they do the task, an essential stage in writing which foreign language learners often ignore.

Have students exchange papers when they have finished. They should compare the different language and ideas they used to handle the same task and at times correct each others' mistakes. This technique helps students to see the strengths and weaknesses of their own work and to improve upon it.

ROUND ONE

Unit One
PEOPLE

1. Read the form. Write down the instructions. Follow the example in number 1.

   1. Please attach photo.

   2.

   3.

   4.

REGISTRAR	Please
MILTON SCHOOL OF ENGLISH	attach
	photo

DO NOT WRITE IN THIS SPACE

PRINT OR TYPE   DO NOT WRITE

TODAY'S DATE _____

1   NAME _____
         Last   First   Middle Name or Initial
                                          (If none, draw line —)

2   AGE _____   3   SEX   ☐ Male   ☐ Female

4   MARITAL STATUS _____

5   NATIONALITY _____

6   OCCUPATION _____

Form IE-5

2. Choose the correct answer.

1. *Print* means

   a. Jane
   b. *Jane*
   c. Jane

2. Jane Stevenson has a husband. What will she write next to *marital status*?

   a. single = never married
   b. married = has a husband or wife
   c. divorced = was married
   d. widowed = was married, husband or wife died

3. What will Jane Stevenson write next to *occupation*?

   a. tennis
   b. Jane Stevenson
   c. teacher

4. What is the last name in *Michael G. Baker*?

   a. Michael
   b. G.
   c. Baker

5. What is the middle initial in *Michael G. Baker*?

   a. Michael
   b. G.
   c. Baker

3. Use this information to fill in the form on page 3.

   The woman's name is Anna Louise Lewis. She's married and has two children. Her husband's American, but she's Canadian. She was born on May 9, 1952. She's a doctor and works in a hospital in downtown Los Angeles.

Listen to a conversation between a secretary and four foreign students. Write down the students' names and where they are from.

	Name	Country
1.		
2.		
3.		
4.		

Fill in the registrar's form with information about yourself.

REGISTRAR	Please
MILTON SCHOOL OF ENGLISH	attach
	photo

DO NOT WRITE IN THIS SPACE

PRINT OR TYPE   DO NOT WRITE

TODAY'S DATE _____

1 NAME _____
           Last   First   Middle Name or Initial
                                        (If none, draw line —)

2 AGE _____   3   SEX ☐ Male   ☐ Female

4 MARITAL STATUS _____

5 NATIONALITY _____

6 OCCUPATION _____

Form IE-5

Fill in the registrar's form on page 6 with information about your partner.

Useful language

What's your name?
How do you spell it?
How old are you?
Are you married?
   Yes, I am.
   No, I'm not.
   No, I'm single.

What's your nationality?
Where are you from?
What do you do?
What type of work do you do?

REGISTRAR **MILTON SCHOOL OF ENGLISH**	Please attach photo

DO NOT WRITE IN THIS SPACE

PRINT OR TYPE   DO NOT WRITE

TODAY'S DATE _____

1 NAME _____
         Last   First   Middle Name or Initial
                                     (If none, draw line —)

2 AGE _____   3 SEX ☐ Male ☐ Female

4 MARITAL STATUS _____

5 NATIONALITY _____

6 OCCUPATION _____

Form IE-5

1. Read the paragraph about Anna Louise Lewis on page 4 again.

2. Write a paragraph about your partner. Begin your paragraph like this:

    My partner's name . . .

Get to know the other students in your class. Talk to them and fill in the questionnaire.

Useful language

What language(s) do you speak? (See page 6.)

Class Questionnaire

Name	Age	Occupation	Country	Language(s)
1.				
2.				
3.				
4.				
5.				
6.				
7.				
8.				
9.				
10.				
11.				
12.				
13.				
14.				
15.				
16.				

Unit Two
AT HOME

1. Look at Text 1. What number should you call for the situations in the pictures? Write the telephone numbers under the pictures. Follow the example in number 1.

1. _922-5523_   2._____   3._____   4._____

2. Read the other sections from the telephone directory. Answer the questions.

1. You want to call Directory Assistance in New Orleans. What number should you call? (Texts 2 and 3)

2. What is the area code for Bangor, Maine? (Text 3)

3. What is Joseph Smith's telephone number? (Text 4)

4. Where does Margaret Sullivan live? (Text 4)

5. Does Rita Sweeney live on North 21st Street or South 21st Street? (Text 4)

6. You want to talk to a man named Smith. He lives on Main Street. What's his telephone number? (Text 4)

Text 1

emergency numbers

dial

Fire or Medical Emergencies		____911
Stop a Crime Save a Life	Philadelphia police	____911
for other police help		____231-3131
Doctor	Office ____	
	Home ____	
Suicide Prevention Center		686-4420
Poison Information Center		____922-5523
Gas Leaks and Emergencies		____235-1212

Water and Sewer Emergencies		____686-3900
Federal Bureau of Investigation	FBI	____629-0800
U.S. Secret Service		____597-0600
U.S. Coast Guard Search & Rescue		____923-4320
Other Important Numbers		_____

Text 2

Directory Assistance

How to call Local Directory Assistance

For numbers within your area code dial:

411

How to call Long Distance Directory Assistance*

For numbers **outside** your area code dial:

1 + Area Code + 555-1212

(Charges vary, depending on your Long Distance Company)

For the telephone numbers of businesses and people who have "800" numbers dial:

1 + 800 + 555-1212

Area Codes

Illinois
Centralia 618
Chicago 312
Peoria 309
Rockford 815
Springfield 217

Indiana
Evansville 812
Indianapolis 317
South Bend 219
Iowa
Cedar Rapids 319
Council Bluffs 712
Des Moines 515

Kansas
Topeka 913
Wichita 316

Kentucky
Ashland 606
Frankfort 502
Louisville 502

Louisiana
Baton Rouge 504
New Orleans 504
Shreveport 318

Maine
all locations 207

Silver Donna	6611 N 52nd St	727 5017
Smith James	4048 E Main St	355 5262
Smith Jos.	108 S 12th St	906 4479
Smith Lisa	1222 S 110th St.	338 5119
Stein D L	4827 W Atlantic Ave	536 8248
Stein Richard	908 N 30th St	266 8844
Stein W	3666 E Crown Ave	473 0029
Sullivan Margaret	5555 W Johnston Rd	924 0963
Sweeney R	630 N 21st St.	829 5737

When people do not know a telephone number, they often call Directory Assistance. Listen to four calls to Directory Assistance. Write down the numbers in the address book.

Name	Area Code	Name	Area Code
Dr. Susan Gold	404	*Jerry Mancini*	215
Street	Phone	Street	Phone
2957 Greenwillow Dr.		*985 Lancaster Ave.*	
City State Zip Code		City State Zip Code	
Atlanta GA 30345		*Philadelphia PA 19010*	

Name	Area Code	Name	Area Code
J. J. Hudson	301	*Mary White*	617
Street	Phone	Street	Phone
1226 Pioneer Rd.		*40 Beacon St.*	
City State Zip Code		City State Zip Code	
Sheridan WY 82801		*Boston MA 02106*	

1. When you are the telephone operator, give the caller the number he or she wants. Begin the conversation like this:

Hello. What city, please?

2. When you are the caller, call up the operator and ask for the telephone numbers of the people on your list. Write the telephone numbers in the address book.

Useful language

I'd like the number for _____ .

Could you give me the number for _____ ?

How do you spell _____ ?

Could you spell _____ ?

Could you repeat the last name, please?

I'm sorry, would you repeat _____ ?

Student A's information is below. Student B will find a different set of information in Appendix A on page 199.

Student A — Operator

Spencer, Paula	860 N Lakeshore Dr	Chicago	445 8011
Spenser, P	1639 W 16th St	Chicago	303 2269
Turner, John	3105 N Kenmore	Chicago	637 4773
Turner, John P	5682 Green Bay Ave	Chicago	883 5447

Student A — Caller

Name *William Browne*	Area Code 206	Name *Rose Chun*	Area Code 206
Street 722 *Cherry*	Phone	Street 3618 *Whitman Ave.*	Phone
City State Zip Code *Seattle WA* 98104		City State Zip Code *Seattle WA* 98103	

STUDENT B: Turn to page 199.

Ask three people in your class for their addresses and telephone numbers. Write them in the address book.

Name	Area Code	Name	Area Code
Street	Phone	Street	Phone
City State Zip Code		City State Zip Code	

Name	Area Code
Street	Phone
City State Zip Code	

Make a class list. Write the names of all the students in your class in alphabetical order. Write down their telephone numbers next to their names.

1. Look at the address on the envelope and the list of abbreviations on page 14.

```
┌─────────────────────────────────────────────────────┐
│  Liz Palmer                                   ┌─────┐ │
│  14 Prince Albert Rd.                         │     │ │
│  London NW1 7SR                               │     │ │
│  UK                                           └─────┘ │
│                                                       │
│                                                       │
│              Mr. Charles Miller                       │
│              10943 Ensbrook Dr.                       │
│              Houston, TX 77099                        │
│              USA                                      │
│                                                       │
└─────────────────────────────────────────────────────┘
```

Abbreviations

Ave.	Avenue	E.	East	CO	Colorado
Dr.	Drive	N.	North	FL	Florida
Rd.	Road	S.	South	MO	Missouri
St.	Street	W.	West		

2. Address three envelopes to these people:

1. Name: Dr. James Henderson
   Address: 900 Bay Drive
   City: Miami Beach
   State: Florida
   Zip Code: 33140

2. Name: Ms. Carol Benson
   Address: 8130 University Drive
   City: St. Louis
   State: Missouri
   Zip Code: 63105

3. Name: Mrs. Margaret Taylor
   Address: 1881 South Grant Street
   City: Denver
   State: Colorado
   Zip Code: 80210

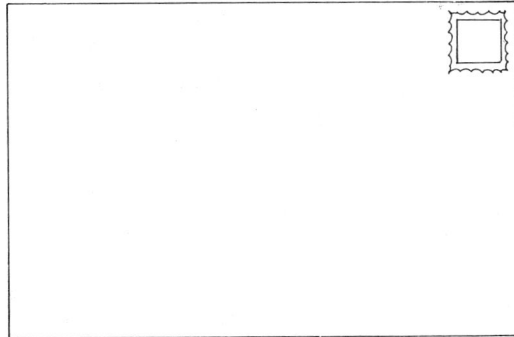

3. Address the fourth envelope to someone in your class.

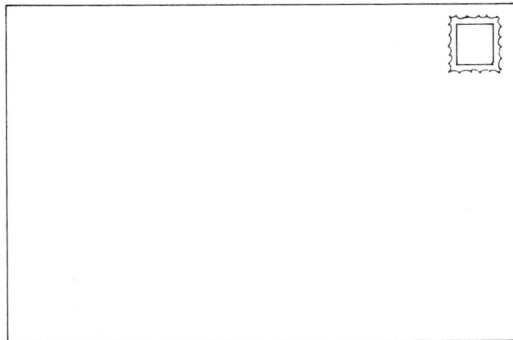

Unit Three
AT HOME

1. Look at the list of words. Then look at the check and telephone bill. Put a mark (✓) next to the words that are in the check or telephone bill.

1. money
2. pay
3. telephone
4. inquiries
5. repair
6. call
7. send
8. tax

2. Match the words on the left with their meanings on the right. Follow the example in number 3.

1. pay   a. questions
2. inquiries   b. to give money
3. repair ―――――――――――――― c. to fix something that is broken
4. call   d. money you give the government
5. tax   e. to telephone

Check 4329

Michael J. Scoulos
Maria Scoulos
701 Maryland Ave
Pittsburgh, Pa. 15232

4329

December 16 19 86

8-28/430

PAY TO THE ORDER OF Hardback Bookstore $ 14 83/100

Fourteen and 83/100 _____ DOLLARS

MEMO Christmas gift   Maria Scoulos

⑈043000261⑈   35ᴵᴵᴵ570   4329

New Jersey Bell

JUL 16, 1983   PAGE   1

BILLING INQUIRIES CALL (609) 347-9950
EMERGENCY REPAIR   CALL   611

A SHORE
S VASSAR SQ & BRDWLK
APT 709
VENTNOR CITY   NJ   08406

MONTHLY SERVICE AND EQUIPMENT-JUL 16 THRU AUG 15 . . . .   10.61
ITEMIZED CALLS 29.37
TAX: FEDERAL 1.20

CURRENT CHARGES   ***DUE BY AUG 8***   41.18

-->101 0906-->615   TOTAL AMOUNT DUE   41.18

17

3. Choose the correct answer.

1. Who is paying the money? (Check)

    a. Michael J. Scoulos
    b. Maria Scoulos
    c. Hardback Bookstore

2. Who is getting the money? (Check)

    a. Michael J. Scoulos
    b. Maria Scoulos
    c. Hardback Bookstore

3. How much is the check for? (Check)

    a. $43.29
    b. $14.83
    c. $1,483

4. When did the person write the check? (Check)

    a. 12/16/86
    b. 3/29/86
    c. 8/26/86

5. When must A. Shore pay the bill? (Telephone bill)

    a. Before August 15th.
    b. On or before August 8th.
    c. On or before July 16th.

6. How much must A. Shore pay? (Telephone bill)

    a. $10.61
    b. $29.37
    c. $41.18

7. A. Shore does not understand the bill. What number should she call?
(Telephone bill)

   a. 611
   b. (609) 347-9950
   c. (609) 823-4978

Make out a check for the telephone bill.

```
                                                            5 1 2

                                    _____19_____      53-471
                                                            113
PAY TO THE
ORDER OF_____  $ [        ]

_____DOLLARS



MEMO_____ _____ _____    _____
1:0113006111:  1084754 211    05
DELUXE CHECK PRINTERS  LH
```

1. Listen to the conversation. Write down how much Jack and Susan spent last month.

Last Month's Expenses

Rent _____

Electricity _____

Phone _____

Water _____

Food _____

Heat _____

Entertainment (Movie, Restaurant) _____

Car (Gas, Insurance) _____

Total _____

2. Listen again. Make out one of the checks they have to pay.

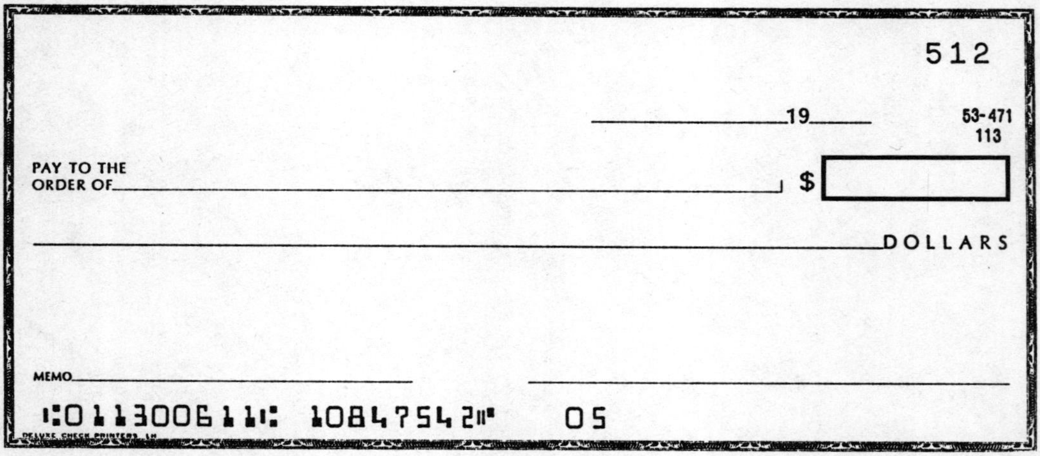

Discuss with your partner(s) how much a family of two needs to live in your city.

Useful language

How much is the average phone bill?

How much does _____ cost?

How much do people need for _____ ?

Rent costs approximately   _____ .

anywhere from   _____ to _____ .

The average water bill is _____ .

Two people need at least _____ for _____ .

Rent   _____   Car

Electricity   _____   (Gas for 300 miles) _____

Phone   _____   (Insurance)   _____

Water   _____   (Other)   _____

Heat   _____   Other

Food   _____   _____ _____

Entertainment   _____   _____ _____

Transportation _____   _____ _____

Total _____

Write down how much you spend in a month.

```
┌─────────────────────────────────────────────────┐
│                 Monthly Budget                  │
│                                                 │
│                                                 │
│                                                 │
│                                                 │
│                                                 │
│                                                 │
│                                                 │
└─────────────────────────────────────────────────┘
```

Ask your partner how much he or she spends in a month. Fill in the budget. Who spends more, you or your partner?

Useful language

How much do you spend on _____ ?

How much is your _____ ?

Is that all you spend?

Boy, you spend a lot on _____ .

Monthly Budget

Unit Four
AT WORK

1. Read the message. Write down the names and dates in it.

Names

a.

b.

c.

Dates

a.

b.

To _Henry Hanson_

Date _5/9/86_   Time _1:10_   A.M. ☐   P.M. ☑

WHILE YOU WERE OUT

M_s._ _Carol Skinner_

of _World Publishers_

Phone _(215) 639 - 4872 x121_

Area Code		Number	Extension
TELEPHONED	✔	PLEASE CALL	
CALLED TO SEE YOU		WILL CALL AGAIN	✔
WANTS TO SEE YOU	✔	**URGENT**	
RETURNED YOUR CALL			

Message _Would like a meeting for next week, May 15th, to talk about the new children's book._

Cathy

Operator

2. Put a T if the statement is true and an F if the statement is false.

1. _____ The person called at 2:15.

2. _____ Carol Skinner called.

3. _____ The person called on Sept. 5, 1986.

4. _____ Ms. Skinner works at World Publishers.

5. _____ Mr. Hanson will call Carol Skinner.

6. _____ Ms. Skinner will call again on May 15th.

7. _____ Cathy is the name of Ms. Skinner's secretary.

Listen to the conversation. Complete the message.

To _Mr. Workman_

Date _____ Time _____ A.M. ☐ P.M. ☐

WHILE YOU WERE OUT

M_____

of_____

Phone_____

Area Code		Number	Extension	
TELEPHONED		PLEASE CALL		
CALLED TO SEE YOU		WILL CALL AGAIN		
WANTS TO SEE YOU		**URGENT**		
RETURNED YOUR CALL				

Message_____

_____

_____

_____

_____

_____

Operator

1. Read the message.

> linda,
>   your mother called at 8:00 this evening
> she and your father can't meet you on
> saturday they're going to washington can
> they meet you next friday instead call her
> tomorrow and let her know *
>   dave

*let her know: tell her.

2. Rewrite the message. Put in capital letters and the correct punctuation.

The sentences in these two conversations are not in the correct order. Put the sentences in the correct order. Follow the example in Conversation 1. Compare your answers with your partner's.

Conversation 1

_____ Secretary: Hold on, please.

_____ Caller: My name is Alice Spencer.

__1__ Secretary: Hello.

_____ Caller: Thank you.

_____ Caller: Hello. I'd like to speak to Mr. Gonzalez, please.

_____ Secretary: Who's calling, please?

Conversation 2

_____ Caller: Hello, can I speak to Mr. Hennessey, please?

_____ Secretary: I'm sorry. He's not here. Can I take a message?

_____ Secretary: Hello.

_____ Caller: Yes, please tell him to call Ray Massey. It's important.

_____ Secretary: And what's your telephone number?

_____ Caller: M A S S E Y.

_____ Caller: Area code 215, 627-9932.

_____ Secretary: How do you spell your last name?

_____ Secretary: Is that M as in Michael?

_____ Caller: Thank you.

_____ Caller: Yes, that's right.

_____ Secretary: All right. I'll give him the message.

1. Listen to the conversations. Check your answers.

2. Repeat the conversations with your partner.

Act out the situations with your partner.

1. When you are the caller, use your "new" name. If the person you call is not there, leave a message. Think of your messages before you call.

2. When you are the secretary, begin the conversation. Say "Hello." If the person is not in, take a message. Be sure to spell the caller's name correctly, and write down the caller's telephone number. When you have finished, show your partner the messages you wrote.

Student A

1. You are the caller. Your name is Mona/Martin Johnson. Your telephone number is 323-6831. Call Mr. Watson.

2. You are the secretary. Ms. Heller is in.

3. You are the caller. Your name is Tina/Ted Block. Your telephone number is (202) 331-5020. Call Ms. Pappas.

4. You are the secretary. Mr. Paulson is not in.

5. You are the caller. Your name is Lisa/Len Hill. Your telephone number is (416) 778-9709, extension 21. Call Joanne Platt.

6. You are the secretary. Mr. Rivers is not in.

STUDENT B: Turn to page 200.

1. Read the note to Linda on page 26 again.

2. Your partner wants to speak to another student in the class. The other student is busy. Your partner will give you a message. Write down the message. Give the message to the other student.

Unit Five
ENTERTAINMENT

1. Look at the ad. Find this information.

   1. Name of the film: _____

   2. Name of the actors: _____

   3. Name of the director: _____

2. Answer the questions.

   1. If you are 16 years old, can you see this movie by yourself?

   2. Can you see the movie today?

   3. At how many theaters can you see this movie?

   4. Does the ad say at what times the film is playing?

   5. Where's the Denis theater? the Cinema World theater?

   6. How much is a ticket for the first show at the Showcase Cinema West?

   7. Is the Showcase Cinema East in Oakland or Monroeville?

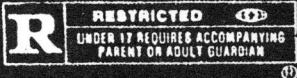

From the MGM release "Year of the Dragon"   ©   1985 Dino de Laurentis Corp.

31

Listen to two phone calls to two movie theaters. Fill in the missing information.

The Manor Twin Cinemas

Squirrel Hill

_____ **Murray Avenue**

421-1628

FIRSTBORN with TERRI GARR	THE LITTLE DRUMMER GIRL with DIANE KEATON and KLAUS KINSKI
Times:	Times:
All tickets: $ _____ _____	All tickets: $ _____ _____
$ _____ All other days	$ _____ All other days

Cinema World   **Route 51 South**   **653-0027**

Year of the Dragon

Times: _____ _____ _____ _____ _____

Tickets: $ _____ 2:00 performance

$ _____ All other performances

1. You and your partner have movie ads, but the ads are for different films. Ask your partner about his or her ads. Fill in your blank ads with the information you get. Decide which film you would like to see.

Useful language

What's playing at the _____ ?
Who's in it?
What's it about?
What times are the performances?

Student A	
OLDIES-BUT-GOODIES WEEK	
ABC	**Center** **TOOTSIE with DUSTIN HOFFMAN, JESSICA LANGE and TERRI GARR.** A comedy about an actor who becomes an actress. 4:30 6:30 8:30 10:30
Bala	**Embassy** **AMADEUS with F. MURRAY ABRAHAM.** A drama about the composers, Antonio Salieri and Mozart. 7:15 9:50

STUDENT B: Turn to page 200.

2. Talk about films to see in your town. Bring in the movie section from a local newspaper if you don't know what movies are playing. Decide which film you and your partner will see.

Useful language

Let's go see _____ .
    Okay. That sounds good.
    All right.

    I've seen it before.
    No, I'm not crazy about (war films).
    I'd rather not. I don't like (war films).

How about (seeing) _____ instead?

What about (seeing) _____ instead?

1. Read the movie ads on pages 33 and 200 again.

2. Make a list of the movies playing in your town.

    a. List the movie theaters in alphabetical order.
    b. Write the names of the movies playing at each theater.
    c. Write the names of the actors and actresses in the films.
    d. Write what the films are about in one or two sentences.

1. Talk to the other students in your group. Find out what they like and don't like. Fill in the questionnaire.

2. Get into new groups. Report the findings of your group questionnaire.

Useful language

Everybody   likes   Nobody likes
Almost everybody   Almost everybody dislikes

Half of the group   likes
More than half
A little more than half of the group
Less than half
A little less than half of the group

Only one person likes
Only two people like

Tom likes _____ , _____ , and _____ , but he

doesn't like _____ or _____ .

Nancy's favorite actor is _____ .

GROUP QUESTIONNAIRE

	Names						

MOVIES

Do you like

love stories?						
war movies?						
comedies?						
musicals?						
westerns?						
science fiction movies?						

MUSIC

pop music?						
country music?						
classical music?						
jazz?						

FAMOUS PEOPLE
Who's your favorite

actor?						
actress?						
singer?						
athlete?						
author?						

✓ = Yes, I do.   0 = Sometimes.   X = No, I don't.
    I like it/them very much.   It's/They're okay.   I don't like it/them at all.

1. Read this report of the first part of a group questionnaire.

Everybody in my group likes love stories, but only one person, Joe Carter, likes war movies. Half of the group likes comedies, and a little more than half of the group likes science fiction movies. Nobody likes musicals, and only two people like westerns.

2. Write a similar report about the type of movies your group likes.

Unit Six
GETTING
SOMEWHERE

1. Look at Map 1. Find these cities as quickly as you can. Are they in the east, west, north, or south?

1. Atlanta
2. Seattle
3. San Diego
4. Milwaukee
5. Miami

6. Detroit
7. Las Vegas
8. Philadelphia
9. St. Louis
10. San Antonio

Map 1

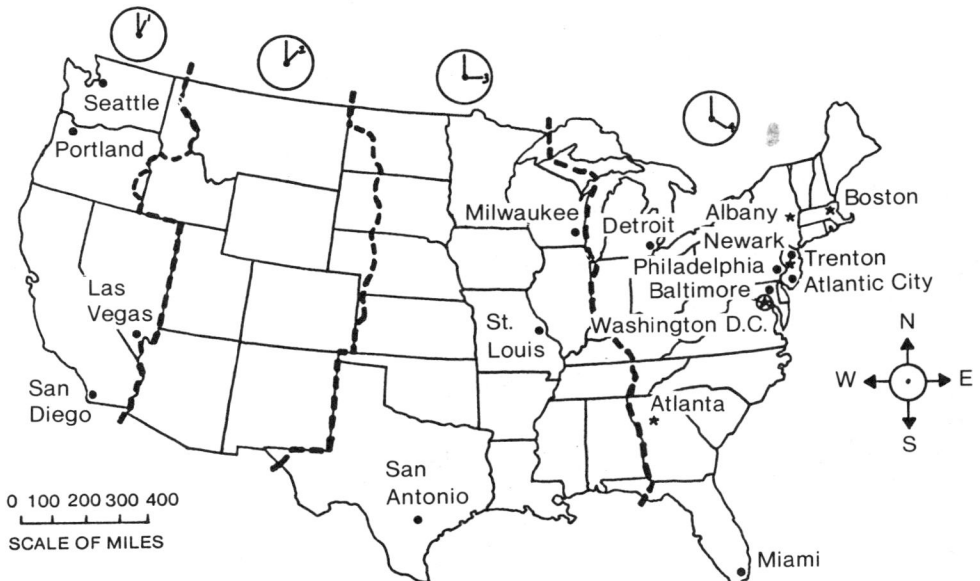

2. Look at Map 2. Are these places east, west, north, or south of San Francisco?

1. Oakland   3. San Francisco International Airport
2. Redwood City   4. Marin County

Map 2

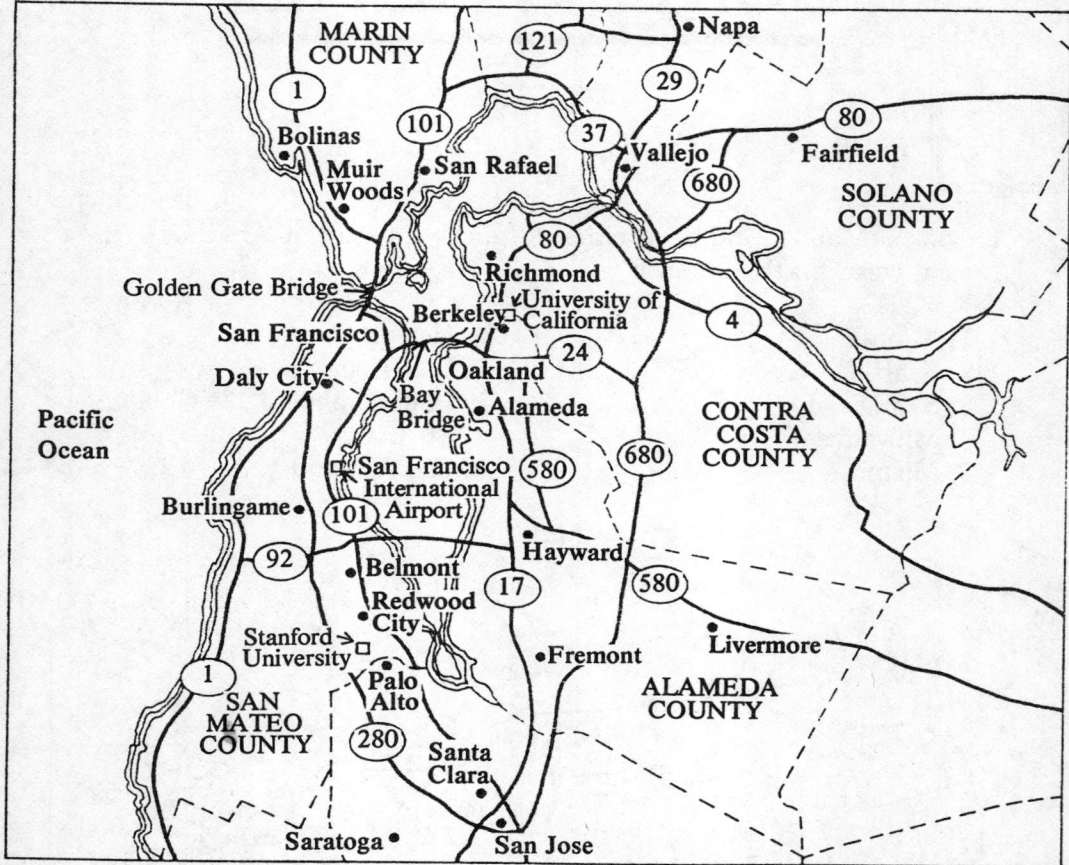

3. Answer the questions. (Map 1)

1. It's 4:00 in Boston. What time is it in Portland?

2. What is the capital of the state of New York?

3. Which state is *not* near Illinois?

   a. Indiana   b. Wisconsin   c. Arkansas   d. Iowa

4. Which city is *not* in New Jersey?

   a. Newark   b. Trenton   c. Atlantic City   d. Baltimore

5. What state is Las Vegas in?

6. How far is Washington, D.C., from Atlanta?

4. You are in San Francisco. Put a T if the statement is true and an F if the statement is false. (Map 2)

1. _____ You want to go to Marin County. You should cross the Bay Bridge.

2. _____ You want to go to the University of California at Berkeley. You should cross the Bay Bridge.

3. _____ San Francisco International Airport is on Route 101.

4. _____ You want to go to Alameda. You should take Routes 101, 92, and 17.

1. Read this paragraph about San Francisco. Fill in the blanks with these words.

and   in   it   of   there

San Francisco is located on the Bay of San Francisco _____

northern California. _____ is about 50 miles from San Jose

_____ 403 miles from Los Angeles. You can get _____

by car, train, bus, _____ plane.

2. Write about your city.

Look at the street map. Mrs. Rivera is new in Pleasantville. Her neighbor, Mrs. O'Malley, is telling her the location of these six places:

hotel	police station	restaurant
movie theater	post office	supermarket

Listen to their conversation. Write the places in the appropriate boxes.

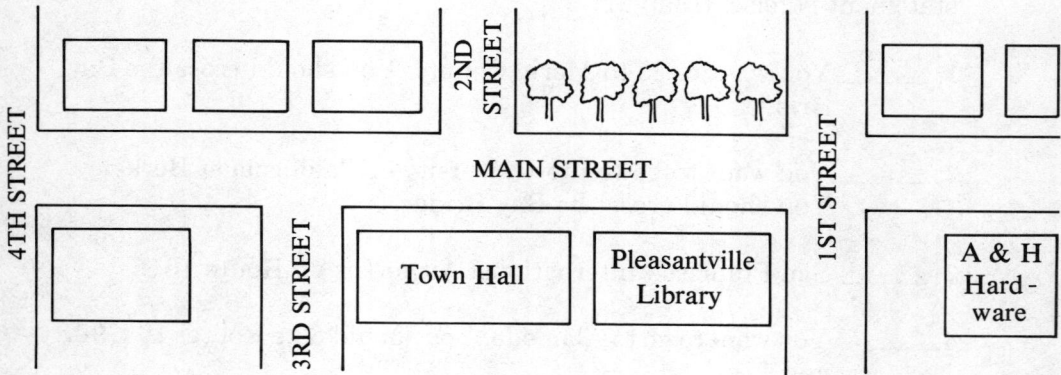

You and your partner have maps of the shopping area of Morristown, but you have different information. Fill in the map. Ask your partner for the information you need.

Useful language

Where's the post office?

It's on _____ Street.

on the corner of _____ and _____ .

between _____ and _____ .

across the street from _____ .

next to _____ .

near _____ .

Student A

Ask your partner for the location of these places:

Anna's Boutique   the post office
World Florist   Bell's Dry Cleaner
Sam's Fruit Store   Market Street Drugstore

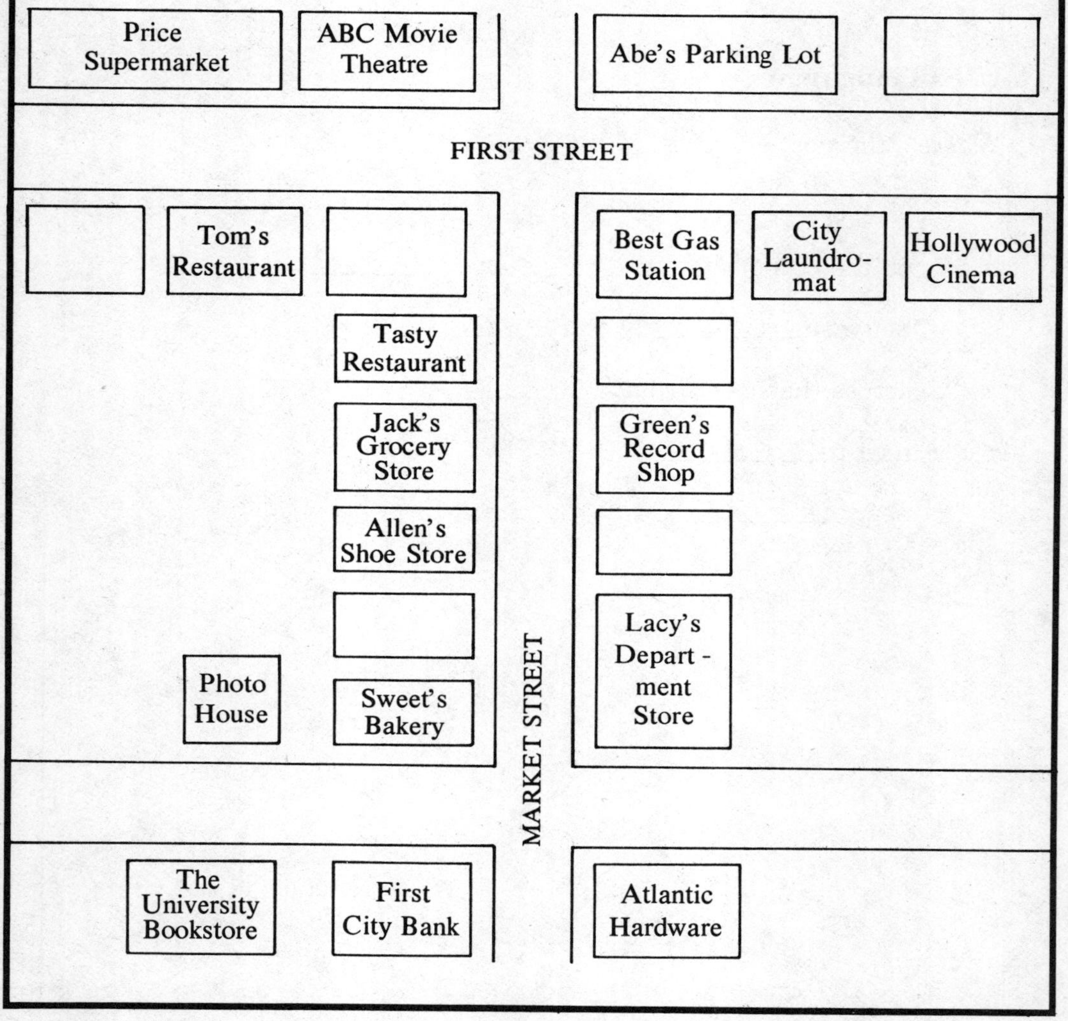

| Price Supermarket | ABC Movie Theatre | | Abe's Parking Lot | |

FIRST STREET

| | Tom's Restaurant | | | Best Gas Station | City Laundro-mat | Hollywood Cinema |

Tasty Restaurant

Jack's Grocery Store

Green's Record Shop

Allen's Shoe Store

| Photo House | Sweet's Bakery |

Lacy's Depart-ment Store

MARKET STREET

| The University Bookstore | First City Bank | | Atlantic Hardware |

STUDENT B: Turn to page 201.

Draw a map of a shopping area near your house. Do not write in the names of the stores. Give the map to your partner. Tell him or her where the stores are. He or she will fill in the map.

Useful language

There's a _____ across the street from my home.

It's called _____ .

The _____ is near the bus stop.

(See page 41 for other expressions.)

1. Read this description of Pleasantville.

   There is a supermarket on the corner of 4th and Main. It's called The Big Apple, and it's across the street from the Town Movie Theater. There's a restaurant near the park on Main Street. It's on the corner of 2nd and Main Streets. There's a hotel between the restaurant and the movie theater. It's called The Flower Hotel, and there are lots of flowers in the front of it. The police station is on the corner of 1st and Main and the post office is next to it.

2. Write a description of your partner's neighborhood. When you have finished, show it to your partner. He or she will tell you if it is correct.

Unit Seven
AWAY FROM HOME

---

1. Look at the train schedule. Find these symbols. Match the symbols on the left with the meanings on the right.

1.   a. You can sleep on the train.

2.   b. Someone will help you with your suitcases.

3.   c. You must reserve a seat a few days before the train leaves.

4.   d. You can get sandwiches and something to drink on the train.

5.   e. You can eat breakfast, lunch, and dinner on the train.

2. Answer the questions. Give the train number.

1. Which trains have sandwiches?

2. Which trains have breakfast, lunch, and dinner?

3. Which trains have beds?

Chicago-Galesburg
West Quincy-Kansas City

347	3	5			Train Number	348	346	4	6
The Illinois Zephyr	The South-west Chief	The Cali-fornia Zephyr			Train Name	The Illinois Zephyr	The Illinois Zephyr	The South-west Chief	The Cali-fornia Zephyr
Daily	Daily	Daily			Frequency of Operation	⑤Ex Su	⑥Su Only	Daily	Daily
⌨	Ⓡ ⬥× ⊞	Ⓡ ⬥×			Type of Service	⌨	⌨	Ⓡ ⬥× ⊞	Ⓡ ⬥×
(BN) 5 55P	(SF) 4 40P	(BN) 2 40P	km 0	Mi 0	(Contracting R.R. As Indicated) Dp **Chicago, IL** -Union Sta. ♿ (CST) Ar	(BN) 10 35A	(BN) 11 50A	(SF) 3 10P	(BN) 4 15P
⊛ 6 13P			22	14	La Grange Road, IL ●	⊛ 9 53A	⊛11 08A		
⊛ 6 36P		⊛ 3 25P	61	38	Aurora, IL	⊛ 9 28A	⊛10 43A		⊛ 3 16P
6 51P			82	51	Plano, IL ●	9 17A	10 32A		
7 17P			133	83	Mendota, IL ● ♿	8 47A	10 02A		
7 37P			168	104	Princeton, IL ●	8 27A	9 42A		
7 59P			211	131	Kewanee, IL ●	8 04A	9 19A		
	5 30P		60	38	Joliet, IL			1 50P	
	6 15P		144	90	Streator, IL			12 56P	
	6 50P		209	130	Chillicothe, IL *(Peoria)* ♿			12 19P	
8 32P	7 35P	5 15P	285 261	177 162	**Galesburg, IL** -N. Broad St. Sta. ● -S. Seminary St. Sta. ♿	7 37A	8 52A	11 33A	1 30P
9 10P			326	202	Macomb, IL ●	6 55A	8 10A		
10 03P			417	258	Quincy, IL ●	6 06A	7 21A		
10 30P			424	263	Ar **West Quincy, MO** ● Dp	6 00A	7 15A		
	8 33P		377	234	Fort Madison, IA			10 38A	
	9 38P		503	312	La Plata, MO ● *(Kirksville)*			9 23A	
	10 15P		558	346	Marceline, MO			8 48A	
	12 05A		725	450	Ar **Kansas City, MO** ♿ *(CST)* Dp			7 10A	

Ar = arrive	A = A.M.	Ex Su = Except Sunday
Dp = depart	P = P.M.	Su only = Sunday only

3. Read these situations. Then read the train schedule. Answer the questions.

1. You want to travel from West Quincy to Chicago. Do you look at the numbers down the left side or up the right side of the schedule?

2. You're going from Kansas City to Chicago. You want to stay in a sleeping car.

   a. What number train do you want?
   b. How long will the trip take?
   c. How far is Kansas City from Chicago?

3. You want to get the early train from Chicago to Galesburg, Illinois.

    a. What time does it leave Chicago?
    b. When does it arrive in Galesburg?

4. It's Monday. You want to go from Galesburg to Chicago. You want the fast train.

    a. What time does the train leave?
    b. How long will the trip take?

5. It's Sunday morning. You want to go from Princeton to Chicago.

    a. What time does the train arrive in Chicago?

1. Listen to three conversations. Where are the speakers: bus station, train station, or airport?

    1.

    2.

    3.

2. Read the conversations. Listen again. Fill in the blanks.

    1. A: Excuse me. What time does the next _____ for Johns-

           town leave?

      B: At _____ .

      A: And what platform does it leave _____ ?

      B: Let's see . . . platform _____ .

      A: And how long _____ the trip _____ ?

      B: About _____ hours.

      A: Thank you.

2. A: Good evening. I have a reservation for this evening's _____ to Guadalajara.

   B: Can I have your _____ , please?

   A: Here you are.

   B: Would you like _____ or nonsmoking?

   A: Nonsmoking, please.

   B: Okay, Here you are, sir. Your seat number is _____ .

   A: Is that in a nonsmoking area?

   B: Yes, it is, sir. Your _____ will be boarding at gate _____ at _____ .

   A: Gate _____ at _____ . Fine. Thank you.

   B: You're welcome, sir. Have a good trip.

3. A: Excuse me. When's the next _____ to Akron?

   B: At _____ .

   A: Can I have _____ tickets, please.

   B: One-way or round-trip?

   A: _____ , please.

   B: That'll be _____ .

   A: Thank you.

   B: You're welcome.

3. Now repeat the conversations with your partner.

47

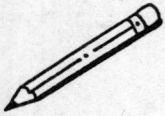

Imagine you are going on one of these trips:

a. a camping trip in the mountains
b. a trip to the Bahamas
c. a trip to New York

Make a list of *all* the things you will need for this trip. Compare your list with your partner's.

1. When you are the customer, get information about buses, trains, and planes. Fill in the chart. Decide how you will go to the place.

2. When you are the travel agent, answer the customer's questions.

	BUS	TRAIN	PLANE	
Frequency				(How often?)
Duration of Trip				(How long?)
Times of Departure				(What time?)
Times of Arrival				(What time?)
Fare				(How much?)

Student A

1. You are in St. Louis. You want to go to Chicago.

2. Your partner is in San Francisco. He or she wants to go to San Diego. This is the travel information:

BUS   Times of Departure 8 AM   12 PM   2 PM   6 PM
              Times of Arrival   4 PM   8 PM   10 PM   2 AM
              Fare (One-way) $28   (Round-trip) $54

TRAIN Times of Departure 9:20 AM   5:45 PM
              Times of Arrival   3:10 PM   11:45 PM
              Fare (One-way) $40   (Round-trip) $75

PLANE Times of Departure 10:05 PM
              Times of Arrival   11:05 PM
              Fare (One-way) $95   (Round-trip) $180

STUDENT B: Turn to page 202.

1. Andrea wrote a note to her friends, George and Helen. Put these parts in the correct order, and write the note in the box on page 50.

   1. Andrea

   2. October 13th

   3. Could you meet me at the station at that time?

4. My train is leaving here at 5:45 PM and arriving in Santa Ana at 11:45.

5. Thanks a lot.

6. I'm coming to Santa Ana on Saturday.

7. Dear George and Helen,

2. Imagine you are going to visit a friend. Write a note. Give the date you are coming and your departure and arrival times, and ask your friend to meet you.

The Traveling Question Game

You and your partner must think of questions people ask at:

   a. airports
   b. bus stations
   c. train stations

Write the questions down. The team that thinks of the most questions is the winner.

Unit Eight
AT SCHOOL

1. Text 1 is from a table of contents (the beginning of a book). Texts 2 and 3 are from indexes (the end of a book). Which text is from

a. an American history book?
b. an American literature book?
c. a cookbook?

Text 1

Table of Contents

Text 2

2. Answer the questions.

1. How many pages are in Chapter 1? (Text 1)

2. What is Chapter 2 about? (Text 1)

3. On what page does Chapter 1 begin? (Text 1)

4. You want to learn how to clean fish. Where should you look? (Text 1)

5. On how many pages can you read about John Quincy Adams? (Text 2)

6. You want to read about the election of John Adams. Where should you look? (Text 2)

7. You want to read about World War II in Africa. Where should you look? (Text 2)

8. You want to read about the characters in Hemingway's books. Where should you look? (Text 3)

9. Where will you *not* read about Hemingway? Find one page number from this list (Text 3): 159, 160, 161, 162, 179, 180, 181, 198, 208.

10. You want to read about *Hiawatha*. Where should you look? (Text 3)

11. What does 259ff. (under *Huckleberry Finn*) mean? (Text 3)

    a. Only on page 259.
    b. On pages 259, 260, and 261.

12. You want to read about the American poet, Langston Hughes. Where should you look in the index? (Text 3)

    a. Before Hemingway.
    b. After Huckleberry Finn.

You and your partner have charts with information about Egypt, Colombia, Thailand, and Senegal, but you have different information. Fill in the chart. Ask your partner for the information you need.

Useful language

What's the population of _____ ?

How big is _____ ?

What's the capital of _____ ?

What's the highest point in _____ ?

What's the longest river in _____ ?

What's the currency in _____ called?

What language(s) do the people speak in _____ ?

What's the major agricultural product of _____ ?

Student A

	Egypt	Colombia	Thailand	Senegal	
Population		27,030,115		5,900,000	
Area		439,828 sq. mi. (1,138,914 km.)	198,242 sq. mi. (517,000 sq.km.)		
Capital	Cairo		Bangkok		
Highest Point			Doi Inthanon 8451 ft. (2,576 m.)	Futa Jallon 1640 ft. (500 m.)	
Longest River	Nile			Senegal	
Currency	Egyptian pound		baht		
Language		Spanish	Thai		
Major agricultural Product	Cotton	Coffee			

STUDENT B: Turn to page 202.

Ask your partner for information about his or her country. Fill in the right-hand column of the chart.

This is a list of homework assignments for a course in English literature. There are some mistakes in it. Listen to the professor of the course. Make the appropriate changes. Some changes have been done for you.

English 201 — The Works of William Shakespeare
Homework Assignments

Week One, 9/18	Introduction to course. The life and times of William Shakespeare.
Week Two, 9/25	*Macbeth*, pages 1–78
Week Three, 10/2	*Macbeth*, pages 56–end
Week Four, 10/9	*Romeo and Juliet*, pages 1–85
Week Five, 10/16	*Romeo and Juliet*, pages 86–end
Week Six, 10/23	Midterm exam
Week Seven, 10/30	*Henry V*, pages 1–59
Week Eight, 11/7	*Henry V*, pages 60–end
Week Nine, 11/14	*Hamlet*, pages 1–69
Week Ten, 11/21	*Hamlet*, pages 70–end
Week Eleven, 11/28	Final exam

People often take notes when they read. They do not copy every word. They only write the important words (usually the verbs, nouns, and adjectives).

1. Read this paragraph about Shakespeare.

William Shakespeare was born in Stratford-upon-Avon, England in 1564. He was a great playwright and poet. Some of his most famous plays were *Hamlet, Macbeth*, and *Romeo and Juliet*. He died in 1616.

2. Make notes from the paragraph. The first sentence has been done for you.

Born Stratford-upon-Avon, 1564

3. Make notes about a writer from your country.

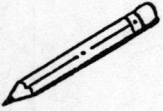

1. Read these notes about the American writer, Ernest Hemingway.

Born Oak Park, Illinois, July 21, 1899. Great novelist and short story writer. *A Farewell to Arms, For Whom the Bell Tolls, The Old Man and The Sea.* Died July 2, 1961.

2. Write a paragraph about Hemingway.

3. Write a similar paragraph about a writer from your country.

Unit Nine
IN THE NEWS

1. These headlines are from six different newspaper articles.
Which article is about:

a. sports? _____

b. a famous person? _____

c. a famous piece of art? _____

d. a place that had a fire? _____

e. a problem at some schools? _____

f. people who are lost? _____

1— Strike Closes Schools

2— *Fire Damages Midtown Building*

3— Trygve Bratteli, Ex-Prime Minister Of Norway, Dies

4— Two Americans Missing In Guatemala Highlands

5— Franks Wins the 400 in 46.27

6— $10.45 million for a painting
Record price paid by Getty museum

2. Answer the questions.

1. Where was Trygve Bratteli from?

2. Who is lost in Guatemala?

3. Are the teachers working?

4. What happened to a building in midtown Manhattan?

5. How much did the Getty museum pay for the painting?

6. Who won the 400-meter race?

3. These are parts from each of the articles. Match the articles with the headlines.

a. _____

OSLO — Trygve Bratteli, 74, a labor leader who survived a Nazi death camp to become prime minister of Norway, died of a brain hemorrhage Tuesday at at Oslo hospital, officials said.

b. _____

LONDON — *Adoration of the Magi*, by Italian Renaissance painter Andrea Mantegna, was sold yesterday to the J. Paul Getty Museum in California for $10.45 million — the highest price ever paid for a painting.

c. _____

The race was the men's 400-meter final, which offered perhaps the day's strongest field. Franks, a 21-year-old Southern Illinois senior from St. Louis, led from the start and beat Antonio McKay of Georgia Tech by 2 meters. Willie McLaughlin of Manhattan, who beat McKay in a semifinal Friday night, finished fourth in the final.

d. _____

More than 200 firefighters — many of whom had to walk up 14 flights of stairs carrying 50 pounds of gear — battled a smoky storage-room fire on the 28th floor of an office tower in midtown Manhattan yesterday morning.

e. _____

According to the United States Embassy here, the two men are Nicholas Blake, 26 years old, a journalist from Pennsylvania, and Griffith Davis, 38, who lives in Guatemala.

f. _____

A strike by more than 200 lay teachers shut down seven of the eight Catholic high schools in South Jersey Tuesday as teachers picketed their schools to pressure for a contract settlement.

4. Look quickly at the articles again. Answer the questions.

1. How old was Trygve Bratteli?

2. What's the name of the painting?

3. Where is Franks from?

4. How many firefighters were there?

5. How old are the two men who are missing?

6. How many schools are closed because of the strike?

The newspaper article below is incomplete.

School On Fire

_____

_____

_____

_____

_____

_____

_____

_____

and parents are worried.

---

1. Read the phrases from the article.

   a. but there were some in their classrooms

   b. A fire broke out* in the kitchen of Mann Elementary School yesterday morning.

   c. Teachers took them out to the playground immediately

   d. There were no children in the school cafeteria at the time

   e. They put the fire out† by 9:10

   f. and parents are worried

   g. Firemen arrived at the school by 8:30

   h. This is the second fire at the school in the past six months

*break out: start   †put out: stop

2. Put the phrases in the correct order. Follow the example in the article.

1. Listen to the news broadcast. The reporter will talk about these subjects:

_____ Sports

_____ International news (news about the world)

_____ Local news (news about the city)

_____ Weather

_____ National news (news about the country)

_____ Medical news (news about health)

Write the number next to the subject in the order that you hear it.

2. Listen again. Choose the correct answer.

1. When is the President's trip to Africa?
   a. March
   b. May

2. Which country is mentioned in the international news?
   a. China
   b. Thailand

3. What is closed because of a strike in Miami?

    a. City schools
    b. City hospitals

4. What is bad for women's health?

    a. Tea
    b. Coffee

5. Who won the game?

    a. Chargers
    b. Wingers

6. What is the temperature?

    a. 51
    b. 71

You and your partner have lists with information about the weather in different cities around the world.

1. Find what the weather was like in these cities.

    1. Your hometown
    2. A city in your country
    3. A city near your country
    4. All other cities on the list

2. Ask your partner for any weather information you don't have.

3. Discuss these questions with your partner.

1. Which city was the hottest?
2. Which city was the coldest?
3. Which city had the best weather?
4. Which city had the worst weather?

Student A

Weather

Abroad

Following are the temperatures and weather conditions in foreign cities yesterday at the local time indicated:

City	Time	Temp	Condition
Aberdeen	1 P.M.	56	Pt.cldy.
Amsterdam	1 P.M.	64	Cloudy
Ankara	3 P.M.		
Athens	2 P.M.	56	Cloudy
Auckland	Mdnt.	67	Rain
Beirut	2 P.M.	68	Clear
Berlin	1 P.M.	58	Pt.cldy.
Bonn	1 P.M.	64	Clear
Brussels	1 P.M.	63	Pt.cldy.
Buenos Aires	9 A.M.		
Cairo	2 P.M.		
Casablanca	Noon	68	Pt.cldy.
Copenhagen	1 P.M.	56	Cloudy
Dakar	Noon	71	Pt.cldy.
Dublin	1 P.M.	54	Cloudy
Geneva	1 P.M.	54	Clear
Helsinki	2 P.M.		
Hong Kong	8 P.M.	71	Cloudy
Jerusalem	2 P.M.	62	Cloudy
Lima	7 A.M.	65	Pt.cldy.
Lisbon	1 P.M.		
London	1 P.M.		
Madrid	1 P.M.	72	Pt.cldy.
Managua	6 A.M.		N.A.
Manila	8 P.M.		
Montreal	1 P.M.	45	Cloudy
Moscow	3 P.M.	44	Clear
New Delhi	6 P.M.	101	Clear
Nice	1 P.M.	62	Cloudy
Oslo	1 P.M.	46	Cloudy
Paris	1 P.M.		
Peking	8 P.M.		
Pretoria	2 P.M.	78	Clear
Rio de Janeiro	9 A.M.	76	Tstrms.
Riyadh	3 P.M.		
Rome	1 P.M.		
Seoul	9 P.M.	47	Clear
Stockholm	1 P.M.	51	Clear
Sydney	10 P.M.	58	Clear
Taipei	8 P.M.		
Tokyo	9 P.M.	59	Clear
Toronto	1 P.M.	43	
Vienna	1 P.M.	60	Pt.cldy.
Warsaw	1 P.M.	55	Clear
Winnipeg	1 P.M.	75	Pt.cldy.

Pt. cldy. = partly cloudy
Tstrms. = thunderstorms

STUDENT B: Turn to page 203.

62

Useful language

sunny		It was hot.
cloudy		warm.
partly cloudy		cool.
rain		cold.
snow		

What was the weather like in _____?

It rained.   There were   showers.
    snowed.   thunderstorms.

1. Read this weather forecast for a city in the United States.

TODAY	Cloudy, changing to partly sunny this afternoon. High in the mid-70s.
TONIGHT	Clear, low around 60.
TOMORROW	Cloudy. Showers and thunderstorms possible. High in the low 70s, low about 60.

2. Write a weather forecast for your city.

"Blondie" is a popular comic strip in American newspapers. Blondie is the woman's name, and Dagwood is the man's.

1. Discuss with your partner what Blondie and Dagwood are saying to each other.

2. Imagine that there is a fifth picture. Discuss with your partner:

   a. what is in this picture
   b. what Blondie and/or Dagwood are saying

ROUND TWO

Unit Ten
PEOPLE

1. This is a letter from Liz to her friend, Penny. The paragraphs are not in order. Read the paragraphs and put them in the correct order.

8/31/86

Dear Penny,

_____   Not much news here. I'm still working at the travel agency though the routine work and same old questions are starting to get to me. Maybe it's time for a change.

_____   Anyway, I'm really looking forward to my vacation. Did I tell you that we're going on a two-week camping trip in the Rockies? It should be great. A completely new experience! I just hope the bears don't get us!

_____   Received your letter today and was glad to hear all is well with you.

_____   Can't think of much else. Hope you are all well and will keep in touch.

_____   Thanks very much for offering to meet my friend, Carmen, at the airport. She's never been to New York before, so it'll be a big help. I hope you'll be able to recognize her. She's about 5'5" tall and is thin. She has short, straight black hair and wears glasses. Maybe you should hold a sign with her name on it so you don't miss each other.

Love,
Liz

2. Put a check (✓) next to the subjects that Liz mentions in her letter.

    1. Her family
    2. Her health
    3. Her work
    4. Her vacation plans
    5. What her friend Carmen looks like
    6. When her friend Carmen is coming

3. Answer the questions.

    1. What does Carmen look like?
    2. Is she very happy with her job?
    3. Where is she going for her vacation?
    4. Is she going by plane?

4. Liz added one sentence to each paragraph. Match the sentences with the correct paragraph.

    1. *I heard that just last week there was one at the campsite we're going to.*

    2. *Just to be safe, I think I'll show her a picture of you so she will know what you look like.*

    3. *I think I'll start looking for a new job after Christmas.*

    4. *It sounds like you really like living in New York.*

    5. *Ben sends you his regards.*

Listen to the telephone conversation between Donna and Ron. Ron is going to pick Donna up to take her to a party. She has never met Ron before. He gives her a description of himself. Which of these pictures is a picture of Ron? What's wrong with the other pictures?

1.  2. 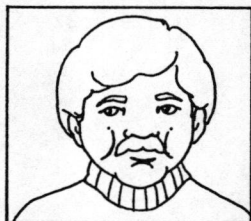 3.  4.

Choose a person from your class to describe. Your partner has to guess who it is. And if your partner cannot guess, say what the person is wearing.

Useful language

She has	short,	straight,	brown	hair.
	long,	wavy,	black	
	medium-length,	curly,	blond	
			gray	
			red	

He is bald.
She has bangs.

He has	brown eyes.
	hazel
	blue

He's	thin.
	average weight.
	a little fat.
	fat/very heavy.

He's 5 feet 8 inches tall.   She weighs about 120 pounds.

She's	short.
	pretty tall.
	medium height.
	tall.

He	wears	glasses.
	is wearing	

He has a	mustache.
	beard.

1. Read this letter from Michael Daly to Mr. Jenkins.

39 Beech Lawn
Dublin 16
September 15th

Dear Mr. Jenkins,
Thank you for offering to pick me up at the airport. It really is very kind of you.
I'll be arriving on Aer Lingus, flight number 602 at 4:30 P.M. I'm about 5'9" tall, and I have short, dark brown hair, blue eyes, and a beard. I'll be wearing a blue shirt, gray sweater, and gray pants. I hope you won't have any trouble finding me.
I'm looking forward to meeting you and your family.

Best wishes,

Michael Daly

2. Imagine that you are taking a trip. Someone has offered to meet you at the airport. Write a short letter and describe yourself.

Do you have dark brown eyes and blond hair? Do you have a beard? Are you 6 feet tall? Are you thin? Are you in your mid-30s? Are you kind and generous? Then you are my dream man.
Sara   Box 877

> Good-looking male, 28, wants to meet intelligent woman in 20s around 5 feet four inches tall with long black hair and blue eyes. Send picture and details to Victor, Box 364.

Are you Sara or Victor's "dream person"? What does your "dream person" look like? How old is he or she? What is more important—looks or personality?

Tell the others in your class about your "dream person." Give as many details as possible. Does anybody in your class have the same "dream person"?

Useful language

My dream	person	is	intelligent.
	man		kind.
	woman		generous.
			polite.
		has	a good sense of humor.

(See page 68 for other expressions.)

1. Read this description.

   My partner is 19 years old. She is abouty five feet six inches tall and weighs around 130 pounds. She has short, straight black hair and has brown eyes. She is wearing a dark blue skirt and white sweater.
   Who is my partner?

2. Write a description of your partner. Do not write his or her name.

3. Your teacher will give your paper to another student in your class. Can he or she guess who your partner is?

Unit Eleven
AT HOME

1. Look at the recipe on page 72. Make a list of the ingredients.

1.

2.

3.

4.

2. Choose the correct answer.

1. *Bring water to a boil* means that the water temperature should be

a. 32°F (0°C)
b. 98.6°F (37°C)
c. 212°F (100°C)

2. What will you use to *cover* the rice?

a.

b.

c.

3. *Simmer* means

a. Cook on a very low fire
b. Cook on a medium fire
c. Cook on a high fire

TO RETAIN VITAMINS, DO NOT RINSE BEFORE OR DRAIN AFTER COOKING

Uncle Ben's®
converted®
Enriched Parboiled   Brand
Rice
natural long grain

Try
COOKING WITHOUT LOOKING
SEE RECIPE
ON BACK

Serving Suggestion

NET WT. 16 OZ. (1 LB.) (454 g)

COOKING DIRECTIONS

1 Bring 2-1/2 cups water to a boil.

2 Stir in 1 cup rice, 1 teaspoon salt, and if desired, 1 tablespoon butter or margarine.

3 Cover tightly and simmer 20 minutes.

4 Remove from heat. Let stand covered until all water is absorbed, about 5 minutes.

Basic recipe (Makes 3 to 4 cups cooked rice *or* 5 to 6 2/3-cup servings):

For SOFTER rice use MORE water and simmer LONGER.

For FIRMER rice use LESS water and simmer for a SHORTER time.

4. To prepare this rice takes

    a. 20 minutes
    b. 25 minutes
    c. More than 30 minutes

5. If you like soft rice, use

    a. Less than 2-1/2 cups of water and cook for more than 20 minutes
    b. More than 2-1/2 cups of water and cook for more than 20 minutes
    c. More than 2-1/2 cups of water and cook for less than 20 minutes

3. Some of these pictures show how to make this rice. The other pictures do not. Cross out the pictures that are incorrect.

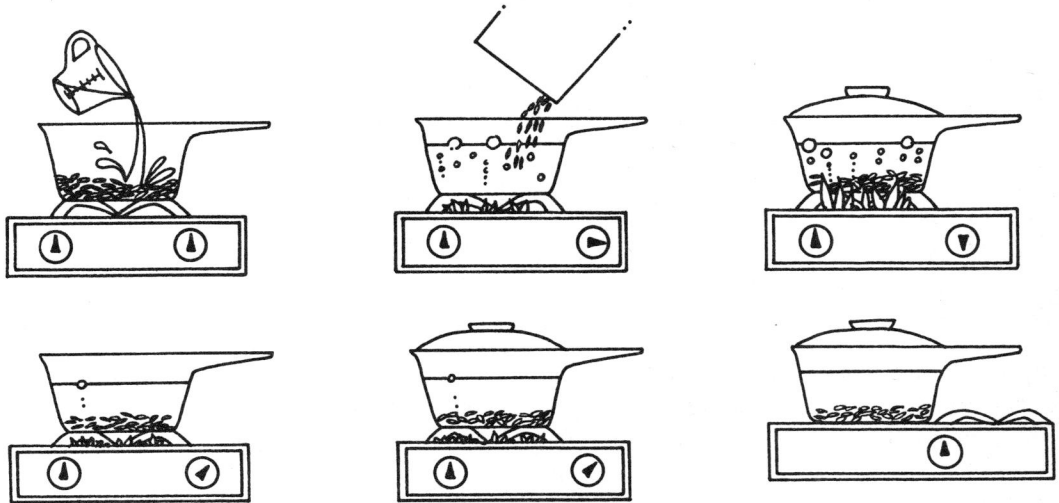

4. How do people in your country make rice?

Listen to the conversation. Fill in the shopping list.

Shopping List

1. _____
2. _____
3. _____
4. _____
5. _____
6. _____
7. _____
8. _____
9. _____
10. _____
11. _____
12. _____

1. Make a list of ten things you like to eat and drink. Imagine that you are at your partner's home. He or she will offer you something to eat and drink. If it is on your list, accept it. If it is not on your list, refuse it.

2. Make a list of ten things that you have at home to eat or drink. Imagine that your partner has come to visit you. Offer him or her the food and drinks on your list.

Useful language

Would you like	an apple?
Can I get you	some juice?
How about	a cup of coffee?

| I'd love | some. |
| | one. |

Yes, please
That sounds good.

| No, | thanks. |
| | thank you. |

You and the members of your group are going to have a party. You are going to invite twenty people. You have $50 to spend. Discuss what you will buy for the party and how much these things will cost.

Write a shopping list for the party.

These pictures show how to make a cheese omelette.

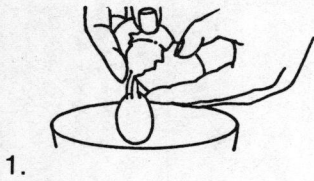

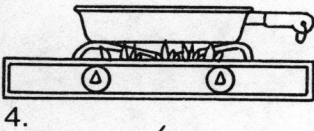

1. 2. 3.

4. 5. 6.

7. 8. 9.

Write a recipe for a cheese omelette.

a. List the ingredients.
b. Describe the method.

Use these words to help you:

break	bowl	eggs
add	fork	salt
beat	pan	pepper
heat	plate	milk
melt		cheese
pour		mixture
fold		
remove		

Unit Twelve
AT HOME

1. Look quickly at the ads. Answer the questions.

1. How many efficiency apartments are for rent?

2. How many 1-bedroom apartments are for rent?

3. How many 2-bedroom apartments are for rent?

4. How many 3-room apartments are for rent?

5. How many 4-room apartments are for rent?

Apts. Rent— Wynnefield

1 5000 blk Gainor Rd. 2 bedrm Duplex. Double baths. $450 mo. + utils. 875-6699 aft 6

Apts. Rent— Overbrook

2 Beautiful 4 rms & bath. 1st fl. $320 mo. Pay own utils. Call TR8-8130 after 5

3 2 bdrms, lg lvrm, newly renov. Reply PO Box 5283, Phila, Pa. 19126

Apts. Rent— Kensington

4 E. York, 2318, kit, br, bth, ww carpt, secure bldg, 1 person. NE4-3603

5 Somerset & "D" St. 1 rm Effic apt. Kitch, pvt bath, 3rd fl, $175 mo. $175 sec deposit. Refs req. Avail immed. 926-6068

Apts. Rent— Northeast

6 BRIDGE & Pratt-1 BR, 2nd fl, ldry connections avail. 298-0498

7 BUSTLETON VIC. 1 bdrm, w/w. A/C. Laundry. No pets. $295. 876-9392

8 DITMAN 6933, 3 rms & bth, refrig, w/w rugs, $230 incl ht & hot water, nr trans. No child/pets 332-2531

9 OXFORD CIRCLE - Duplex, walking distance to everything, 2nd fl. Call 698-2883

10 OXFORD CIR 2nd flr, 1 BR, mod bth & kit, w/w $260+. 698-9581

11 TORRESDALE Avenue - 2 Bedroom, modern kitchen & bath, wall to wall carpet, 2nd floor, private entrance, adults preferred. $325/Month. 824-2018.

See next page for a list of abbreviations and definitions.

Abbreviations

aft = after
apt = apartment
avail = available
bedrm/br = bedroom
bth = bath
effic = efficiency
fl/flr = floor
ht = heating
incl = including/included
kit/kitch = kitchen

lg = large
lvrm = living room
mo = month
mod = modern
nr = near
pvt = private
rms = rooms
trans = transportation
utils = utilities

2. Choose the correct answer.

1. *Utilities* (Ads 1 and 2) means

   a. Large rooms
   b. Heat and water

2. An *efficiency* (Ad 5) means

   a. One big room, kitchen, and bath
   b. A living room, bedroom, kitchen, and bath

3. *No pets* (Ad 7) means

   a. No animals
   b. No children

4. *Including heat and hot water* (Ad 8) means

   a. You pay more for heat and hot water
   b. You do not pay more for heat and hot water

5. *Near transportation* (Ad 8) means

   a. Near stores and schools
   b. Near buses and subway stops

6. *$260+* (Ad 10) means

   a. $260
   b. More than $260

3. Fill in the chart with the correct information.

	Location	Number of bedrooms	Floor	Rent	Telephone or Address for reply
Ad 1			✕		
Ad 2	✕				
Ad 3	✕		✕		
Ad 4			✕		
Ad 5					
Ad 6				✕	
Ad 7			✕		
Ad 8		✕			
Ad 9		✕		✕	
Ad 10	✕				
Ad 11					

Listen to Jeannie Campbell's conversation with a real estate agent. Write down the information she finds out.

1. Rent:

2. What floor the apartment is on:

3. Number of bedrooms:

4. Number of bathrooms:

5. What day she can see it:

6. Time:

7. Address:

This is an empty living room. In groups decide where to put the furniture and other objects.

Useful language

Why don't we _____ ?   We could _____ .

Let's put _____ .

Can we move _____ ?

Yeah, I like that idea.
That sounds good.
That'll look nice.

No, I don't think that's a good idea.
No, I'm not crazy about that idea.
That'll look terrible.

1. Read this description of a living room. Draw a picture of it.

My living room is not very large, but it's comfortable. We have a big oval-shaped carpet in the middle of the room. The sofa is against one wall, and the TV and stereo are against the opposite wall. There's an end table to the left of the sofa and next to the wall, and there's a coffee table in front of the sofa. We also have two armchairs on each side of the coffee table. They are facing the sofa.

The stereo is to the right of the TV, and there's a big plant on the floor to the left of the TV. We have two bookcases. One is above the TV, and the other is above the stereo. There's a mirror between the two bookcases.

2. Write a description of your living room. Give the description to your partner. He or she will draw a picture of your living room according to your description.

Imagine that you want to rent your home. Write an ad to put in an English-language newspaper. You should include:

    a. the town or neighborhood your home is in
    b. the number of bedrooms
    c. the rent
    d. who to call
    e. the phone number

You may also include:

    a. the size
    b. the good points about your home (for example, is it near the center of town, or does it have a big garden?)
    c. restrictions (for example, no pets)
    d. what time or days to call
    e. any other information you think is important

1. Imagine that you are looking for a place to live. Your partner's home is for rent. Read his or her ad. Ask for more information. Ask when you can see it. Write down all the information.

2. Imagine that you want to rent your home. After your partner reads your ad, give him or her any other information he or she wants.

Useful language

What's the rent?
How much is the rent?

How big is _____ ?
   It's 180 square feet.

Is | there | a _____ ?
Are | | any _____ ?

Does it have | a _____ ?
             | any _____ ?

How many _____ are there?

When can I _____ ?

   How about Friday?

   Why don't you come on _____ ?

Can I see it this week?
   Sure.
   I'm afraid I can't this week.

Unit Thirteen
AT WORK

1. Look at the job application on page 84. In which of the categories would you find the following information?

CATEGORY

1. Your name   a. <u>Personal information</u>

2. Another job you have had   b. _____

3. Date of graduation from high school   c. _____

4. The name and address of a person who knows you   d. _____

5. Your social security number   e. _____

6. The type of job you want   f. _____

2. Fill in the application with the following information.

1. The applicant's name is Barbara Ann Lewis.

2. She lives at 1212 Scott Street, Arlington, Va. 22132.

3. She doesn't speak any foreign language fluently, but she can read French well.

APPLICATION FOR EMPLOYMENT
(PRE-EMPLOYMENT QUESTIONNAIRE)   (AN EQUAL OPPORTUNITY EMPLOYER)

PERSONAL INFORMATION

DATE

NAME

SOCIAL SECURITY
NUMBER

LAST   FIRST   MIDDLE

PRESENT ADDRESS

STREET   CITY   STATE   ZIP

PERMANENT ADDRESS

STREET   CITY   STATE   ZIP

PHONE NO.   ARE YOU 18 YEARS OR OLDER   Yes ☐   No ☐

Height _____ feet _____ inches   Weight _____ lbs.

What Foreign Languages do you speak fluently? _____ Read _____ Write _____

EMPLOYMENT DESIRED

POSITION

DATE YOU
CAN START

SALARY
DESIRED

ARE YOU EMPLOYED NOW?

IF SO MAY WE INQUIRE
OF YOUR PRESENT EMPLOYER?

EVER APPLIED TO THIS COMPANY BEFORE?   WHERE?   WHEN?

EDUCATION	NAME AND LOCATION OF SCHOOL	*NO. OF YEARS ATTENDED	*DID YOU GRADUATE?	SUBJECTS STUDIED
GRAMMAR SCHOOL				
HIGH SCHOOL				
COLLEGE				
TRADE, BUSINESS OR CORRESPONDENCE SCHOOL				

FORMER EMPLOYERS (LIST BELOW LAST FOUR EMPLOYERS, STARTING WITH LAST ONE FIRST).

DATE MONTH AND YEAR	NAME AND ADDRESS OF EMPLOYER	SALARY	POSITION	REASON FOR LEAVING
FROM				
TO				
FROM				
TO				
FROM				
TO				
FROM				
TO				

REFERENCES: GIVE THE NAMES OF THREE PERSONS NOT RELATED TO YOU, WHOM YOU HAVE KNOWN AT LEAST ONE YEAR.

	NAME	ADDRESS	BUSINESS	YEARS ACQUAINTED
1				
2				
3				

"I CERTIFY THAT THE FACTS CONTAINED IN THIS APPLICATION ARE TRUE AND COMPLETE TO THE BEST OF MY KNOWLEDGE AND UNDERSTAND THAT, IF EMPLOYED, FALSIFIED STATEMENTS ON THIS APPLICATION SHALL BE GROUNDS FOR DISMISSAL.

I AUTHORIZE INVESTIGATION OF ALL STATEMENTS CONTAINED HEREIN AND THE REFERENCES LISTED ABOVE TO GIVE YOU ANY AND ALL INFORMATION CONCERNING MY PREVIOUS EMPLOYMENT AND ANY PERTINENT INFORMATION THEY MAY HAVE, PERSONAL OR OTHERWISE, AND RELEASE ALL PARTIES FROM ALL LIABILITY FOR ANY DAMAGE THAT MAY RESULT FROM FURNISHING SAME TO YOU.

I UNDERSTAND AND AGREE THAT, IF HIRED, MY EMPLOYMENT IS FOR NO DEFINITE PERIOD AND MAY, REGARDLESS OF THE DATE OF PAYMENT OF MY WAGES AND SALARY, BE TERMINATED AT ANY TIME WITHOUT ANY PRIOR NOTICE."

DATE   SIGNATURE

4. She wants to work as a computer programmer. She can begin in two months and wants to make at least $33,000 a year.

5. She studied mathematics at the University of North Carolina in Chapel Hill from 1979 to 1983.

6. Since graduating from college, she has had two jobs. The first was at First City Bank, 2436 D Street, N.W. in Washington, D.C. She was an assistant computer programmer there and made $19,000 a year. She worked there for only two years after college because the job wasn't interesting. She currently works at the Southern Tool Company, 900 S. Joyce, as a computer programmer. She's been working there since she left her first job. She likes her job, but is not paid well. She only makes $25,000 a year.

Fill in the application on page 86 with information about yourself.

Listen to two people talk about the work they do. Guess their jobs. Write down the words that helped you guess.

1. Job:

   Clues:

2. Job:

   Clues:

What's My Line?

Choose a job. The other students have to guess this job. They can ask you (up to) twenty questions. Answer only with "yes" or "no." If they cannot guess the job, they lose and you win.

APPLICATION FOR EMPLOYMENT
(PRE-EMPLOYMENT QUESTIONNAIRE)　　(AN EQUAL OPPORTUNITY EMPLOYER)

PERSONAL INFORMATION

DATE

NAME

SOCIAL SECURITY NUMBER

　　　　　LAST　　　　FIRST　　　MIDDLE

PRESENT ADDRESS

　　　　　　　STREET　　　　　　　　CITY　　　　　　　STATE　　　ZIP

PERMANENT ADDRESS

　　　　　　　STREET　　　　　　　　CITY　　　　　　　STATE　　　ZIP

PHONE NO. _____　　　　　　ARE YOU 18 YEARS OR OLDER　Yes ☐　　No ☐

Height _____ feet _____ inches　　Weight _____ lbs.

What Foreign Languages do you speak fluently? _____ Read _____ Write _____

EMPLOYMENT DESIRED

POSITION

DATE YOU CAN START

SALARY DESIRED

ARE YOU EMPLOYED NOW?

IF SO MAY WE INQUIRE OF YOUR PRESENT EMPLOYER?

EVER APPLIED TO THIS COMPANY BEFORE?　　WHERE?　　　　　　WHEN?

EDUCATION	NAME AND LOCATION OF SCHOOL	*NO. OF YEARS ATTENDED	*DID YOU GRADUATE?	SUBJECTS STUDIED
GRAMMAR SCHOOL				
HIGH SCHOOL				
COLLEGE				
TRADE, BUSINESS OR CORRESPONDENCE SCHOOL				

FORMER EMPLOYERS (LIST BELOW LAST FOUR EMPLOYERS, STARTING WITH LAST ONE FIRST).

DATE MONTH AND YEAR	NAME AND ADDRESS OF EMPLOYER	SALARY	POSITION	REASON FOR LEAVING
FROM				
TO				
FROM				
TO				
FROM				
TO				
FROM				
TO				

REFERENCES: GIVE THE NAMES OF THREE PERSONS NOT RELATED TO YOU, WHOM YOU HAVE KNOWN AT LEAST ONE YEAR.

	NAME	ADDRESS	BUSINESS	YEARS ACQUAINTED
1				
2				
3				

"I CERTIFY THAT THE FACTS CONTAINED IN THIS APPLICATION ARE TRUE AND COMPLETE TO THE BEST OF MY KNOWLEDGE AND UNDERSTAND THAT, IF EMPLOYED, FALSIFIED STATEMENTS ON THIS APPLICATION SHALL BE GROUNDS FOR DISMISSAL.

I AUTHORIZE INVESTIGATION OF ALL STATEMENTS CONTAINED HEREIN AND THE REFERENCES LISTED ABOVE TO GIVE YOU ANY AND ALL INFORMATION CONCERNING MY PREVIOUS EMPLOYMENT AND ANY PERTINENT INFORMATION THEY MAY HAVE, PERSONAL OR OTHERWISE, AND RELEASE ALL PARTIES FROM ALL LIABILITY FOR ANY DAMAGE THAT MAY RESULT FROM FURNISHING SAME TO YOU.

I UNDERSTAND AND AGREE THAT, IF HIRED, MY EMPLOYMENT IS FOR NO DEFINITE PERIOD AND MAY, REGARDLESS OF THE DATE OF PAYMENT OF MY WAGES AND SALARY, BE TERMINATED AT ANY TIME WITHOUT ANY PRIOR NOTICE."

DATE　　　　　　　　　　SIGNATURE

Useful language

Do you _____ ?

Do you have to know how to _____ ?

Do you have to _____ ?

Do you have to be able to _____ ?

Read this job description.

First of all, an English language teacher should know English very well. In addition, she should like working with other people. She should also be good at helping people with things they do not understand. Finally, a good teacher should always be understanding and patient.

What skills and characteristics do these jobs require?

Use the suggestions in the boxes or any other characteristics you can. Discuss it with your partner.

be good at

working with numbers

selling things

working at heights

talking to people   giving financial* advice

typing

speaking on the phone

working with his or her hands

*financial: having to do with money

be

strong

friendly

imaginative

organized

like to

work alone

travel

work in an office

work outdoors

Useful language

A _____ should | like to   _____ .

             must | be good at

                      | be

I don't agree. A _____ doesn't have to _____ .

I don't think a _____ has to _____ .

Don't you think a _____ | should _____ ?

                                 | has to _____ ?

I think it's more important for a _____ to _____ than it is

for a _____ .

1. Read the job description on page 87 for an English language teacher again.

2. Write a job description for a secretary, traveling salesperson, accountant, or construction worker. Use these words:

        First of all   In addition   also   Finally

3. Write another description for a job you know well.

Unit Fourteen
ENTERTAINMENT

1. What does the TV page *not* tell you? (Choose one.)

1. The times the programs are on.

2. The channels the programs are on.

3. The programs that are good for children.

4. What the programs are about.

2. Answer the questions.

1. What channel is *Star Search* on?

2. What kind of program is *Benny Hill*?

3. What time does *Wembley Music Festival* begin?

4. What year was *Santa Fe Trail* made?

5. Who is in *The Man Who Would Be King*?

6. What time will *The Reincarnation of Peter Proud* finish?

7. Which film does *not* take place in the United States?

8. If you want to hear rock music, what program should you watch?

3. Which program would you watch?

Saturday

11:25 PM to 11:30 PM

11:25 (A&E) LITTLE MIKE—Documentary
A profile of space-shuttle ground technician Michael Anderson, who is 3 feet 6 inches tall.

11:30 ② STAR SEARCH—Talent Contest
Guests: Isabel Sanford and Christopher Atkins. (60 min.)

④ MOVIE—Thriller
"The Amityville Horror." (1979) James Brolin and Margot Kidder team in an adaptation of Jay Anson's best seller about a Long Island family coping with the supernatural. (2 hrs., 10 min.)

⑥ ⑪ ㉑ SATURDAY NIGHT LIVE
Host: George Carlin, who last appeared on SNL in its debut (Oct. 11, 1975). Also: rock group Frankie Goes to Hollywood. (Live; 90 min.)

⑦ BENNY HILL—Comedy
Benny returns from a safari with an unusual trophy.

⑨ WEMBLEY MUSIC FESTIVAL
Patrick Duffy hosts this country-music show set in London. Guests include Emmylou Harris, B.J. Thomas, the Osmond Brothers, Lee Greenwood, David Frizzell and Shelly West. Music: "Jose Cuervo" (Shelly). (60 min.)

⑩ BENNY HILL—Comedy
Benny does a sketch from the life of an imaginary famous musician.

⑲ MOVIE—Drama (BW)
"Santa Fe Trail." (1940) Rousing adventure of six U.S. Army officers and their fight against John Brown's abolitionists in pre-Civil War Kansas. Errol Flynn. (2 hrs.)

㉗ BENNY HILL—Comedy
Benny plays a newscaster.

㉝ MOVIE—Adventure
"The Man Who Would Be King." (1975) Sean Connery and Michael Caine play lusty soldiers of fortune in director John Huston's entertaining version of this Rudyard Kipling story, filmed in Morocco. (3 hrs.)

㊵ FORERUNNER—Variety

(43C) THREE STOOGES—Comedy (BW)

㊺ MOVIE—Thriller
"The Reincarnation of Peter Proud." (1975) Michael Sarrazin as a tormented college instructor who suspects that he previously lived as a man murdered 28 years earlier. Jennifer O'Neill. (2 hrs.)

(CBN) JOHN ANKERBERG—Religion

A-40 TV GUIDE

Pittsburgh Metropolitan Edition

1. Listen and put a check (✓) next to the program Charlie and Rosita decide to watch.

    a. *Star Search*
    b. *The Amityville Horror*
    c. *Saturday Night Live*
    d. *Benny Hill*

    e. *Wembley Music Festival*
    f. *Santa Fe Trail*
    g. *The Man Who Would Be King*
    h. *The Reincarnation of Peter Proud*

2. Listen again. Write down in note form why they do not watch the other programs. Cross out the one they watch.

    a. *Star Search*
    b. *The Amityville Horror*
    c. *Saturday Night Live*
    d. *Benny Hill*

    e. *Wembley Music Festival*
    f. *Santa Fe Trail*
    g. *The Man Who Would Be King*
    h. *The Reincarnation of Peter Proud*

Make a list of the TV programs that will be on TV in your town tonight. Use the TV schedule on page 91 as a model. Include:

    a. the time
    b. the channel
    c. the type of program
    d. the actors/performers
    e. what the program is about

You and your partner are going to watch TV together. Use your TV schedule or your partner's. Decide what you will watch, and list the programs in the chart.

Useful language

Why don't we watch _____ ?

Let's watch _____ .
   Okay.
   Yeah. That sounds good.

I'd rather not. I don't like _____ . Why don't we watch_____
   instead?

If you don't mind, I'd rather watch _____ .

Time				
Program				
Channel				

This is a scene from a cowboy movie.

1.

2.

3.

4.

1. Discuss with your partner what the people are saying. Write the dialogue in the balloons.

2. Tell the story of what happened at the Silver City Bank. Use these words to help you:

   Last Monday Mrs. Olsen / bank. She / want / bank manager. Bill Garrity / there too. He / some money. Everything / quiet. Suddenly / masked man / enter. He / gun. Everyone / afraid. He / teller / "   ." Teller / the safe. Just at that moment / Mrs. Olsen / bag of beans up in the air. Bank robber / surprised. He / up. Bill immediately / gun. He / bank robber / "   ." Mrs. Olsen / smile. She / know beans had stopped / robbery. Bank manager / "   ."

Write what happened at the Silver City Bank. Add a few sentences of your own to finish the story.

Unit Fifteen
GETTING SOMEWHERE

1.

SHADYSIDE

SHADYSIDE PARKING

0–1 HR. $1	
1–2 HRS. $2	
ALL DAY $3.50	
NITE RATE $2	
SAT. ALL DAY $4	

2.

DO NOT TALK TO DRIVER
WHILE BUS IS IN MOTION

3.

MAXIMUM SPEED
55
MINIMUM SPEED
40

4.

PLEASE STAY
WITH YOUR CAR
UNTIL ATTENDANT
TAKES YOUR KEYS

5.

OFFICIAL RATES
$1.35 FIRST MILE
20¢ ea. add. MILE
20¢ ea. add. PERSON

ea add. = each additional

6.

RING BUZZER ONE BLOCK BEFORE STOP

7.

STREET
CLEANING

NO PARKING
IN THIS BLOCK
TUESDAY
9AM TO 1PM
APR 1 TO NOV 30

8.

THIS TAXICAB IS AUTHORIZED TO
COLLECT AN ADDITIONAL CHARGE OF
50¢ PER TRIP (NOT PER PASSENGER)
ON ALL RIDES
COMMENCING BETWEEN 8PM AND 6AM

1. Look at the signs. Write down the number of the sign next to the place where you usually see it.

a. In a taxi   _____   _____

b. On a bus   _____   _____

c. At a parking lot _____   _____

d. On a road   _____   _____

2. Choose the correct answer.

1. *Additional* (Sign 5) means

   a. more
   b. less

2. *Maximum* (Sign 3) means

   a. biggest
   b. smallest

3. *Attendant* (Sign 4) means

   a. a person who works at a parking lot
   b. you, the driver

4. *Buzzer* (Sign 6) means

   a. telephone
   b. bell

5. (Sign 1) How much will parking from 1 PM to 6 PM cost?

   a. $2.00
   b. $5.00
   c. $3.50

6. (Sign 2) When can you talk to the driver?

   a. When he or she is driving
   b. When the bus is stopped
   c. All the time

7. (Sign 5) How much does a taxi ride of 3 miles cost?

    a. $1.75
    b. $3.35
    c. $4.15

8. (Sign 3) How fast should you drive on this road?

    a. Faster than 55 miles per hour
    b. Faster than 40 miles per hour
    c. Slower than 40 miles per hour

9. (Sign 7) When can you *not* park your car on this road?

    a. On Tuesday, June 1st, from 2 PM to 8 PM
    b. On Tuesday, January 1st, from 9 AM to 1 PM
    c. On Tuesday, July 1st, from 10 AM to 12:30 PM

10. (Sign 8) You are with a friend. It is 11 PM. The meter says $5.60. How much do you have to pay?

    a. $5.60
    b. $6.10
    c. $6.60

Listen to the conversation. Mark the route on the map.

You and your partner are at the bus stop. Give him or her directions to a place on the map. Do not say the name of the place. Your partner has to guess.

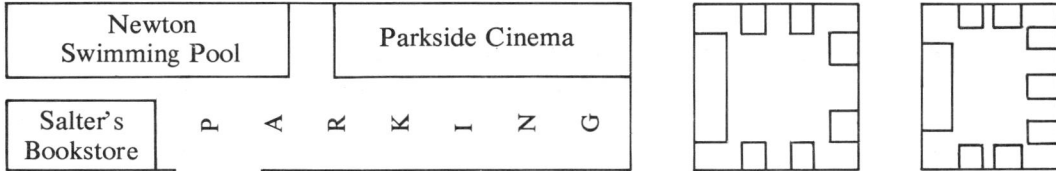
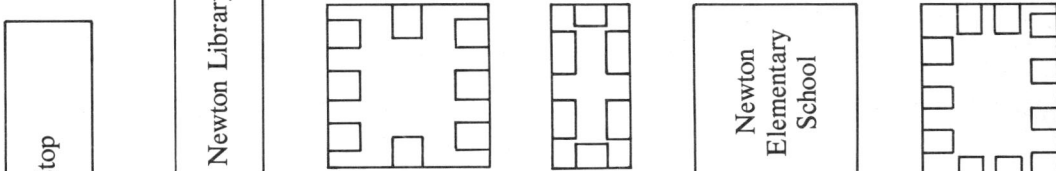
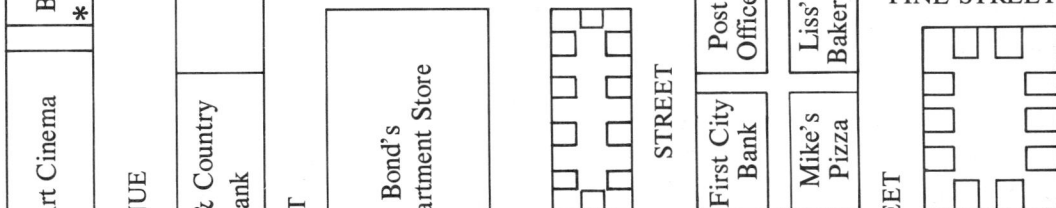
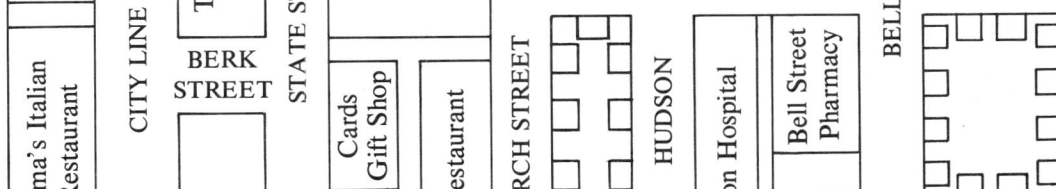

Useful language

Go	up	City Line Avenue.		Turn	left	at Westside Highway.
	down	this street.			right	the third street.

Go straight until you come to	Westside Highway.
	the first traffic light.
	a bank.

Cross the street.

It's the first building on	the	left.
	your	

Look at the map on page 99 again.

1. Draw a map of your neighborhood. Draw boxes for the various places, but do not write in the names of the places.

2. Give your partner your map. Tell him or her how to get to your house from the nearest bus or subway stop. He or she will mark in the route on your map.

3. Your partner will ask you for directions to different places in your neighborhood. He or she will mark in the routes on the map.

Useful language

How do I get to a bank from your house?

Excuse me, can you tell me where the nearest drugstore is?

1. Read these directions. Mark the route on the map on page 99.

When you come out of the subway, you'll be on the corner of State Street and Westside Highway. Turn left and walk down State until you pass Bond's Department Store. Turn right there and walk two blocks down Pine. At Hudson make a right and then make a left at the next corner. You'll see a bank on one side of the street and a hospital on the other. Walk down one block and make another left. My house is the second one on the right before you get to Pine.

2. Now write directions from the house to the subway stop. Use the map on page 99 to help you.

Write directions to your house from the nearest bus or subway stop. Give your directions to your partner. He or she will mark in the route on your map.

Unit Sixteen
AWAY FROM HOME

1. Write down your three favorite kinds of food.

   a.

   b.

   c.

   Look at the menu. Does the restaurant have any of your favorite food?

2. Write down the sections where you will find the prices for these items. Number 3 has been done for you.

   1. A cold roast beef sandwich _____

   2. A hot roast beef sandwich _____

   3. A cold roast beef sandwich with three pieces of bread

      Triple Decker Sandwiches _____

   4. A hamburger _____

   5. French fried potatoes _____

   6. Milk _____

   7. Small amounts of food _____

From The Grill

Open Faced Grilled Cheese with
Bacon, Tomato and French Fries . 3.00
Grilled Swiss Cheese 1.80
   with Tomato 2.05
   with Ham OR Bacon 2.90
Pork Roll 1.75
   with Melted Cheese 2.10
Fried Egg Sandwich 1.20
   with Bacon OR Ham 2.10
   with Pork Roll 2.20
Western Egg Sandwich 2.20
Grilled Cheese 1.60
   with Tomato 1.80 with Tuna ... 2.80
   with Bacon OR Ham 2.70
Reuben Sandwich 3.85
Fried Ham Sandwich 2.20
Frankfurter 1.50

Hamburger 1.60
Cheeseburger 1.70
Deluxe Hamburger 2.85
Deluxe Cheeseburger 2.95
California Hamburger 1.85
California Cheeseburger ... 2.00
Bacon Cheeseburger 2.65
Pizza Burger 2.10
Meat Ball Sandwich 2.45

TOMATO 20¢ EXTRA

Soups

Soup Du Jour	Cup .70	Bowl .90
Clam Chowder	Cup .70	Bowl .90

Sandwiches

Roast Beef 2.90
Roast Turkey 2.90
Baked Virginia Ham 2.85
Boiled Ham 2.35
Boiled Ham and Cheese 2.85
American Cheese 1.55
Swiss Cheese 1.70
Boiled Ham and Swiss Cheese 2.90
Tuna Fish Salad 2.35
Chicken Salad 2.25
Shrimp Salad 2.80
Egg Salad 1.65
Bacon, Lettuce and Tomato 2.20

Salad Platters Crispy Cold

IMPORTED BONELESS, SKINLESS SARDINES .. 5.45
COTTAGE CHEESE with Peaches or Fruit Salad . 5.35
INDIVIDUAL CAN of SALMON 5.75
HOMEMADE CHOPPED LIVER 4.75
COLD SLICED ROAST TURKEY 6.35
COLD SLICED ROAST BEEF 6.35
CHEF'S JULIENNE BOWL 6.35
GREEK SALAD 6.35
COLD JUMBO WHOLE SHRIMP 6.95
TUNA FISH SALAD 5.45
SHRIMP SALAD 5.75
CHICKEN SALAD 5.20

Triple Decker Sandwiches

PLEASE ORDER BY NUMBER

1. Sliced Turkey, Bacon, Lettuce and Tomato 4.75
2. Virginia Ham, Swiss Cheese, Lettuce and Tomato 4.65
3. Roast Beef, Bacon, Lettuce and Tomato 4.75
4. Tuna Fish, Sliced Egg, Lettuce and Tomato 4.75
5. Chicken Liver, Bacon, Lettuce and Tomato 4.55

SERVED WITH COLE SLAW

Hot Open Sandwiches

HOT ROAST SIRLOIN of BEEF or ROAST TURKEY 4.95
HOT ROAST TURKEY, All White Meat 5.25
HOT BAKED VIRGINIA HAM 4.95
HOT ROAST FRESH HAM 4.95

SERVED WITH CHOICE OF VEGETABLE AND POTATOES

Childrens Corner

PLEASE ORDER BY ANIMAL NAME

LION - SLICED TURKEY, Veg. & Potato 3.55
ELEPHANT - HAMBURGER, French Fries & Cole Slaw 2.85
DONKEY - FRANKFURTER with Potato 2.00
MOOSE - HOT BEEF SANDWICH, Veg. & Potato 3.55
BEAR - SPAGHETTI with One Meat Ball (Complete) 2.85
ZEBRA - GRILLED CHEESE with French Fries 2.25

Side Orders

French Fried or Mashed
  Potatoes .... .95
French Fried Onion Rings . 1.60
Cole Slaw 1.00
Potato Salad 1.00
Cottage Cheese 1.00
Lettuce and Tomato 1.05
Vegetables of Today 1.00

Desserts

Ice Cream, Single 1.00
Ice Cream, Double 1.50
Strawberry Shortcake 1.45
Cheese Cakes 1.60
Layer Cakes 1.30
Assorted Fruit Pies ... 1.00
  Ala Mode 1.50
Assorted Cream Pies ... 1.15
  Ala Mode 1.50
Jello with Whipped Cream ... 1.00
Fruit Salad 1.20
Creamy Rice or Chocolate Pudding 1.10
Melons (in season) 1.20
Danish Pastry .... .75
Apple Turnovers 1.00

Beverages

Coffee .... .40		Coke, Large .... .70
Tea .... .35		Iced Coffee .... .70
Milk .... .75		Iced Tea .... .70
Sanka .... .50		Diet Soda .... .70
Hot Chocolate .. .65		
Orange Juice	.65	.90
Grapefruit Juice	.65	.90
Pineapple Juice	.65	.90
Tomato Juice	.65	.90
Prune Juice	.65	.90

103

3. Find the prices on the menu.

1. How much is a small glass of orange juice and a deluxe cheeseburger with tomato?

2. How much is a grilled cheese with bacon?

3. How much is an open faced grilled cheese with tomato, bacon, and french fries?

4. How much is a hot turkey sandwich with french fries?

5. How much is a cup of clam chowder, a frankfurter, french fries, and a hot cup of tea?

6. How much is a grilled cheese for a child, french fries, and a Coke?

4. Choose the correct answer.

1. *Deluxe* (Deluxe Hamburger) probably means

   a. big
   b. small

2. *Soup du Jour* means

   a. chicken soup
   b. a different soup every day

3. You want a triple decker tuna fish sandwich. You say

   a. "I'd like a triple decker tuna fish sandwich, please."
   b. "I'd like a number four, please."

4. You want a frankfurter for a child. You say

   a. "Can I have a donkey, please?"
   b. "Can I have a frankfurter and potato, please?"

5. What comes with the cold roast beef platter? (Salad Platters Crispy Cold)

   a. Lettuce, tomato, egg, and cole slaw.
   b. The menu doesn't say.

1. Listen to the conversation between a waitress and two customers.

    a. Write down what the customers order.

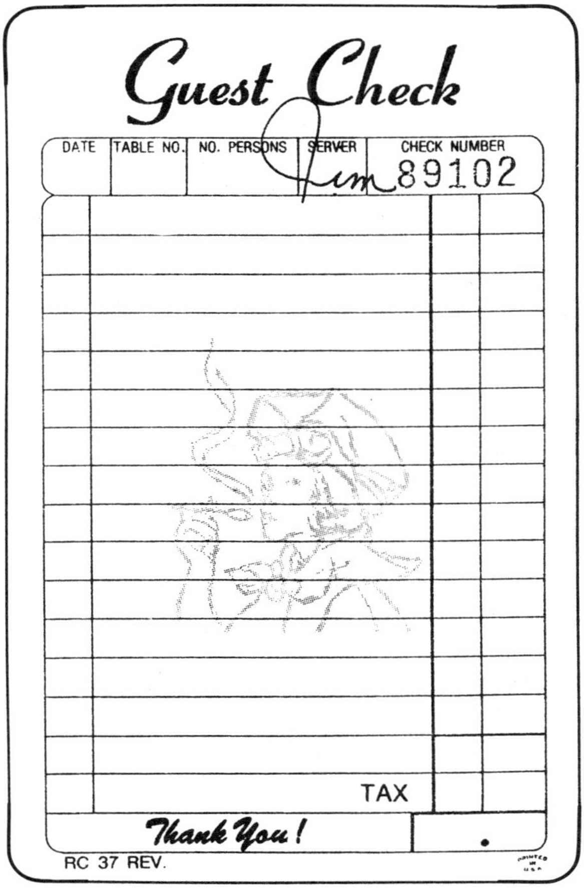

DATE	TABLE NO.	NO. PERSONS	SERVER	CHECK NUMBER

Guest Check

Server: *Jim* Check Number: **89102**

TAX

Thank You!

RC 37 REV.

    b. Look at the menu on page 103 again. How much will their bill be?

2. Listen again. Write down the complete questions that the customers and waitress ask.

1. _____ _____ _____ soup _____ _____ _____ _____ ?

2. _____ _____ drink?

3. _____ _____ _____ _____ _____ a pizza burger _____ ?

4. _____ _____ the tuna fish salad platter _____ _____ ?

5. _____ _____ _____ any dessert?

6. _____ _____ _____ _____ water _____ ?

In groups of three take turns at being customers in a restaurant and the waiter or waitress.

Student A

Waiter/Waitress

Give the menu to your customers. Answer any of their questions. Write down what they order.

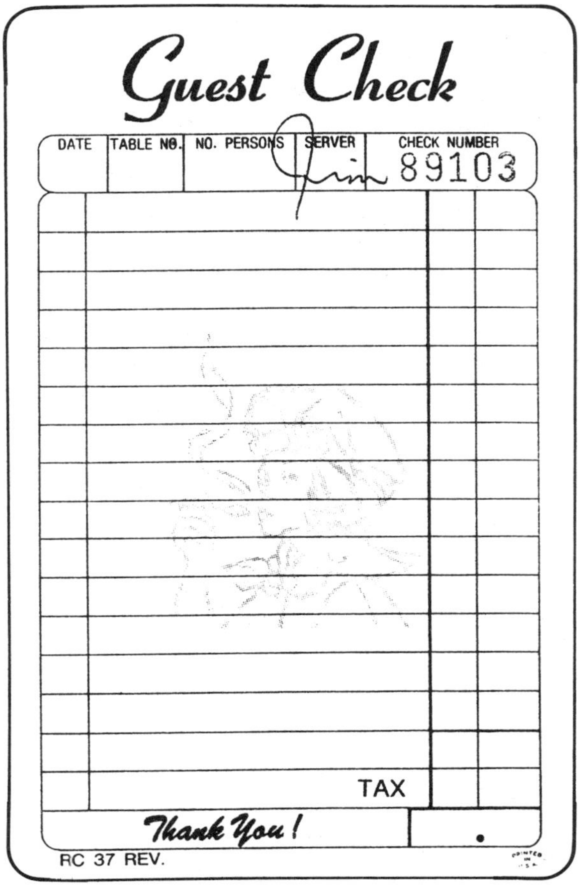

Guest Check				
DATE	TABLE NO.	NO. PERSONS	SERVER	CHECK NUMBER 89103

TAX

Thank You!

RC 37 REV.

STUDENT B: Turn to page 204.

Useful language

Are you ready to | order?
May I take your |

What would you like to _____ ?

Would you like anything _____ ?

A pizza burger is | a hamburger with tomato sauce and cheese.
                  | made with tomato sauce and cheese.

It's | a little | spicy.
     | not too |
     | very |

It's very good.
You'll like it very much.

Tony and Sheila received this card from some friends. The rain ruined some of the card.

1. Read the card.

2. Fill in all the missing parts.

Photo provided courtesy of Government of India Tourist office.

May 22 nd

Tony and Sheila,
   Having a wonderful time here in
         Everything is so interesting
The food is great.   night we   in a
great restaurant.   had the most wonderful
fish dishes. We really   the one with
shrimps,   matoes ice and all sorts of
unusual spices.   other dishes were also
good   some were a little too hot for us.
Hope   are all well. We miss   both.
                         Love,
                           Sandy & Gary

Imagine that you are a tourist in your country or in another country. Write a postcard to a relative or friend.

The Restaurant Game

What you need:

1. A different object to move along the board for each player—for example, a coin, a paper clip, a key.

2. A die *or* six pieces of paper. If you use pieces of paper, write one number (from 1 to 6) on each piece, and turn them over.

START HERE →

Ask for a menu. **1**	Say how you like your eggs. **2**	Order something for breakfast. **3**	Ask for some more water. **4**	Write down the names of three vegetables. **5**

Complain about the soup. Be polite. **6**

Ask what kind of ice cream the restaurant has. **7**

Order something for lunch. **8**

Say that you would like lettuce and tomato on your hamburger. **9**

Complain about your steak. Be polite. **10**

Write down the names of three desserts. **11**

TOUGH

WEAK

SALTY

Not done enough

COLD

STRONG

TOO WELL DONE

You've won! Hope you enjoy your free meal. **20**

Excuse me! I think . . .

Excuse me! I'm afraid . . .

Say that there's a mistake in the bill. Say what the mistake is. **19**

Ask about the price of a cup of coffee. **18**

Ask for the bill. **17**	Describe a national dish from your country. **16**	Ask if the restaurant serves beer. **15**	Write down the names of four kinds of fruit. **14**	Complain about the coffee. Be polite. **13**

Ask what the restaurant has for dessert. **12**

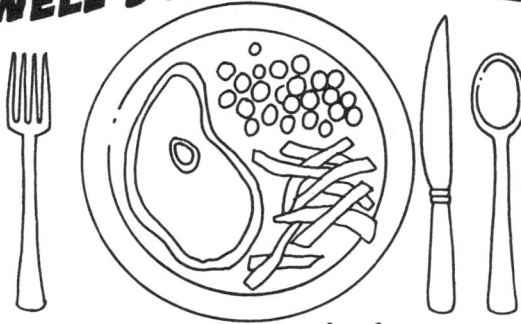

111

The rules:

1. Throw the die or choose a piece of paper with a number on it. (After each player's turn, remember to mix up the pieces of paper.)

2. Move the correct number of squares.

3. Do what the instructions on the square say.

4. If you cannot do it or the other players think you have made a mistake, then you miss a turn.

5. The first player to land *on* 20 is the winner. If you get a number that is too big for you to land on 20, then you must go back to the beginning and start again. For example, if you are on 19 and you get a 1, then you win. But if you get a 2, you go back to square 1. If you get a 3, you go back to square 2, and so on.

Optional:

One person in the group can be secretary and write down what the players say for each square. At the end of the game you can compare notes with the other groups.

Unit Seventeen
AT SCHOOL

1. Put these words in alphabetical order.

1. result
2. rest
3. respond
4. requirement
5. reserve
6. reporter
7. return
8. responsible
9. research
10. restaurant

2. Look at the dictionary page on page 114. Answer the questions.

1. Which of these words is *not* on this page?

   a. rose
   b. roomy
   c. rondo

2. The last word on the page is *root*. You say it like this: $r\overline{oo}t$ or $r\breve{oo}t$. Where can you find what the symbols — and ⌣ mean?

3. What are the abbreviations for these words?

   noun
   verb
   adjective
   adverb
   plural

Ro·ma·ni·an (rō-mā′nē-ən, -mān′yən) *adj. & n.* Variant of **Rumanian.**

Ro·man·ic (rō-măn′ĭk) *adj.* 1. Of or derived from the ancient Romans. 2. Romance. —**Ro·man′ic** *n.*

Ro·man·ism (rō′mə-nĭz′əm) *n.* Roman Catholicism.

Ro·man·ist (rō′mə-nĭst) *n.* 1. One who professes Roman Catholicism. 2. A student of or authority on Roman law, culture, and institutions.

Ro·man·ize (rō′mə-nīz′) *tr.v.* **-ized, -iz·ing, -iz·es.** 1. To convert (someone) to Roman Catholicism. 2. To make Roman in character, allegiance, or style. 3. To write or transliterate in the Latin alphabet. —**Ro′man·i·za′tion** *n.*

Roman law *n.* The system of laws of ancient Rome, upon which the legal systems of many countries are based.

Roman nose *n.* A nose with a high, prominent bridge.

Roman numeral *n.* Any of the numerals formed with the characters I, V, X, L, C, D, and M in the ancient system of numeration.

Ro·ma·no (rə-mä′nō, rō-) *n.* A hard, dry Italian cheese similar to but sharper than Parmesan. [Ital., Roman < Lat. *Romanus.*]

Ro·mans (rō′mənz) *pl.n. (used with a sing. verb).* See table at **Bible.**

Ro·mansch also **Ro·mansh** (rō-mänsh′, -mänsh′) *n.* The Rhaeto-Romanic dialects of eastern Switzerland and neighboring parts of Italy. [Romansch *Romantsch* < Lat. *Romanicus,* Roman. —see ROMANCE.]

ro·man·tic (rō-măn′tĭk) *adj.* 1. Of, pertaining to, or characteristic of romance. 2. Given to thoughts or feelings of romance. 3. Conducive to romance. 4. Imaginative but impractical: *romantic notions.* 5. Not based on fact; imaginary. 6. Of or characteristic of romanticism in the arts. —*n.* 1. A romantic person. 2. A romanticist. [Fr. *romantique* < OFr. *romans,* romance.] —**ro·man′ti·cal·ly** *adv.*

ro·man·ti·cism (rō-măn′tĭ-sĭz′əm) *n.* 1. An artistic and intellectual movement that originated in the late 18th century and stressed strong emotion, imagination, freedom from classical correctness in art forms, and rebellion against social conventions. 2. The spirit and attitudes characteristic of romantic thought. —**ro·man′ti·cist** *n.*

ro·man·ti·cize (rō-măn′tĭ-sīz′) *v.* **-cized, -ciz·ing, -ciz·es.** —*tr.* To interpret romantically. —*intr.* To think in a romantic way. —**ro·man′ti·ci·za′tion** *n.*

Ro·ma·ny (rŏm′ə-nē, rō′mə-) *n., pl.* **-nies.** 1. A Gypsy. 2. The Indic language of the Gypsies. [Romany *romani,* pl. of *romano,* gypsy < *rom,* man < Skt. *ḍomah,* man of a low caste.] —**Rom′a·ny** *adj.*

ro·maunt (rō-mônt′, -mŏnt′) *n. Archaic.* A verse romance. [ME < OFr. *romant,* romance < Lat. *Romanicus,* Roman. —see ROMANCE.]

Ro·me·o (rō′mē-ō′) *n., pl.* **-os.** A male lover. [After *Romeo,* the hero of *Romeo and Juliet* by William Shakespeare (1564–1616).]

Rom·ish (rō′mĭsh) *adj.* Of or pertaining to the Roman Catholic Church. —**Rom′ish·ly** *adv.* —**Rom′ish·ness** *n.*

romp (rŏmp) *intr.v.* **romped, romp·ing, romps.** 1. To play or frolic boisterously. 2. *Slang.* To win easily. —*n.* 1. Lively, merry play; frolic. 2. One, esp. a girl, that sports and frolics. 3. *Slang.* An easy win. [Alteration of RAMP[2].]

romp·er (rŏm′pər) *n.* 1. One that romps. 2. **rompers.** A loose-fitting playsuit with short bloomers worn esp. by small children.

Rom·u·lus (rŏm′yə-ləs) *n. Rom. Myth.* The son of Mars and legendary founder of Rome. [Lat.]

ron·deau (rŏn′dō, rŏn-dō′) *n., pl.* **-deaux** (-dōz, -dōz′). 1. A lyrical poem of French origin having 13 or sometimes 10 lines with two rhymes throughout and with the opening phrase repeated twice as a refrain. 2. *Mus.* A monophonic trouvère song. [OFr., alteration of *rondel.* —see RONDEL.]

ron·del (rŏn′dəl, rŏn-dĕl′) *n.* A rondeau that usually has 14 lines. [ME < OFr., dim. of *ronde,* circle, round. —see ROUND.]

ron·de·let (rŏn′dl-ĕt′, -dl-ā′) *n.* A short rondeau having five or seven lines and one refrain in one stanza. [OFr., dim. of *rondel,* rondel.]

ron·do (rŏn′dō, rŏn-dō′) *n., pl.* **-dos.** A musical composition having a refrain that occurs at least three times in its original key between contrasting couplets. [Ital. *rondò* < OFr. *rondeau,* rondeau.]

ron·dure (rŏn′jər, -dyŏŏr′) *n.* Something circular or gracefully rounded. [OFr. *rondeur,* roundness < *ronde,* round. —see ROUND.]

ron·nel (rŏn′əl) *n.* 1. A solid, light-brown compound, C₈H₈Cl₃O₃PS, used as an insecticide, esp. against flies and cockroaches. 2. **Ronnel** A trademark for ronnel outside the United States. [< *Ronnel,* a non-U.S. trademark.]

rönt·gen (rĕnt′gən, -jən, rŭnt′-) *n.* Variant of roentgen.

rood (rŏŏd) *n.* 1. **a.** A crucifix symbolizing the cross on which Christ was crucified. **b.** A large crucifix or the representation of one over the altar or rood screen of a medieval church. 2. *Chiefly Brit.* A measure of length that varies from 5½ to 8 yards. 3. A measure of land equal to ¼ acre, or 40 square rods. [ME < OE *rōd.*]

rood screen *n.* An ornamented altar screen, usually surmounted by a crucifix, separating the choir of a church from the nave.

roof (rŏŏf, rŏŏf) *n.* 1. The exterior surface and its supporting structures on the top of a building. 2. The top covering of something: *the roof of a car.* 3. **a.** A vaulted inner structure: *the roof of the mouth.* **b.** The highest point; summit: *the roof of the world.* 4. A house or home. —*tr.v.* **roofed, roof·ing, roofs.** To furnish or cover with or as if with a roof. —*idiom.* **raise the roof.** *Slang.* 1. To be extremely noisy and boisterous. 2. To complain loudly and bitterly. [ME < OE *hrōf.*]

roof·er (rŏŏf′ər, rŏŏf′ər) *n.* One who lays or repairs roofs.

roof garden *n.* 1. A garden on the roof of an urban building. 2. A restaurant at the top or on the roof of a building that often features music and dancing.

roof·ing (rŏŏf′ĭng, rŏŏf′ĭng) *n.* Materials used in building a roof.

roof·less (rŏŏf′lĭs, rŏŏf′-) *adj.* 1. Lacking a roof. 2. Having no home or shelter; homeless.

roof·top (rŏŏf′tŏp′, rŏŏf′-) *n.* The surface of a roof, esp. a flat roof.

roof·tree (rŏŏf′trē′, rŏŏf′-) *n.* 1. A long horizontal beam extending along the ridge of a roof; ridgepole. 2. A roof.

rook[1] (rŏŏk) *n.* **a.** A crowlike Old World bird, *Corvus frugilegus,* that nests in colonies near the tops of trees. —*tr.v.* **rooked, rook·ing, rooks.** *Slang.* To swindle. [ME *rok* < OE *hrōc.*]

rook[2] (rŏŏk) *n.* A chess piece that may move in a straight line over any number of empty squares in a rank or file. [ME *rook* < OFr. *roc* < Ar. *rukh* < Pers.]

rook·er·y (rŏŏk′ə-rē) *n., pl.* **-ies.** 1. **a.** A place where rooks nest and breed. **b.** The breeding ground of certain other birds and animals, such as seals. 2. *Informal.* A crowded and run-down tenement.

rook·ie (rŏŏk′ē) *n. Slang.* 1. An untrained recruit. 2. A novice player in sports. 3. An inexperienced person. [Alteration of RECRUIT.]

room (rŏŏm, rŏŏm) *n.* 1. A space that is or may be occupied by something: *a desk that takes up too much room.* 2. **a.** An area separated by walls or partitions from other similar parts of the structure or building in which it is located. **b.** The people present in such an area: *The whole room laughed.* 3. **rooms.** Living quarters. 4. Suitable opportunity: *room for error.* —*intr.v.* **roomed, room·ing, rooms.** To occupy a room; lodge. [ME *roum* < OE *rūm.*]

room and board *n.* Lodging and meals either earned or provided.

room·er (rŏŏm′ər, rŏŏm′ər) *n.* A lodger.

room·ette (rŏŏm-ĕt′, rŏŏm-ĕt′) *n.* A small private compartment in a railroad sleeping car.

room·ful (rŏŏm′fŏŏl′, rŏŏm′-) *n., pl.* **-fuls.** 1. As much or as many as a room will hold. 2. The number of people in a room.

rooming house *n.* A house where lodgers may rent rooms.

room·mate (rŏŏm′māt′, rŏŏm′-) *n.* A person with whom one shares a room or apartment.

room·y (rŏŏm′ē, rŏŏm′ē) *adj.* **-i·er, -i·est.** Having plenty of room; spacious. —**room′i·ly** *adv.*

roor·back (rŏŏr′băk′) *n.* A false or slanderous story used for political advantage. [After Baron von *Roorback,* imaginary author of an imaginary book, *Roorback's Tour Through the Western and Southern States,* from which a passage was purportedly quoted in an attempt to disparage presidential candidate James K. Polk in 1844.]

roost (rŏŏst) *n.* 1. A perch on which domestic fowl or other birds rest or sleep. 2. A place with perches for fowl or other birds. 3. A place for temporary rest or sleep. —*intr.v.* **roost·ed, roost·ing, roosts.** To rest or sleep on or as if on a perch or roost. —*idiom.* **rule the roost.** To be in charge; dominate. [ME *rooste* < OE *hrōst.*]

roost·er (rŏŏs′tər) *n.* 1. **a.** The adult male of the common domestic fowl. **b.** The adult male of other birds; cock. 2. A pugnacious and cocky person.

root[1] (rŏŏt, rŏŏt) *n.* 1. **a.** The usually underground portion of a plant that serves as support, draws food and water from the surrounding soil, and stores food. **b.** A similar underground plant part such as a rhizome, corm, or tuber. **c.** One of many small, hairlike growths that serve to attach and support plants such as the ivy and other vines. 2. The embedded part of an organ or structure such as a hair, tooth, or nerve. 3. A base or support. 4. An essential part or element; basic core: *finally got to the root of the problem.* 5. A primary source; origin. 6. An antecedent or ancestor. 7. Often **roots.** The condition of being settled and of belonging to a particular place or society: *put down roots in a new town.* 8. *Ling.* An element that constitutes the basis from which a word is derived by phonetic change or by the addition of other elements, such as inflectional endings or affixes. 9. *Math.* **a.** A number that when multiplied by itself an indicated number of times forms a product equal to a specified number: *a fourth root of 4 is* $\sqrt{2}$. **b.** A number that reduces a polynomial equation in one variable to an identity when it is substituted for the variable. **c.** A root *a* of the polynomial equation *f(x)* = 0 in which (*x-a*) occurs at least twice as a factor of *f(x).* 10. *Mus.* **a.** The note from which a chord is built. **b.** The first or lowest note of a triad or chord. —*v.* **root·ed, root·ing, roots.** —*intr.* 1. To grow a root or roots. 2. To become firmly established, settled, or entrenched. —*tr.* 1. To cause to put out roots and grow. 2. To

I	1
II	2
III	3
IV	4
V	5
VI	6
VII	7
VIII	8
IX	9
X	10
XI	11
XII	12
XIII	13
XIV	14
XV	15
XVI	16
XVII	17
XVIII	18
XIX	19
XX	20
XXI	21
XXIX	29
XXX	30
XL	40
XLVIII	48
IL	49
L	50
LX	60
XC	90
XCVIII	98
IC	99
C	100
CI	101
CC	200
D	500
DC	600
CM	900
M	1,000
MDCLXVI	1666
MCMLXXX	1980

Roman numeral

ă pat / ā pay / âr care / ä father / b bib / ch church / d deed / ĕ pet / ē be / f fife / g gag / h hat / hw which / ĭ pit / ī pie / îr pier / j judge / k kick / l lid, needle / m mum / n no, sudden / ng thing / ŏ pot / ō toe / ô paw, for / oi noise / ou out / ŏŏ took / ōō boot /

3. Answer the questions.

1. What is the plural of *rondeau*?

2. What is the adverb of *romantic*?

3. What does the *o* in *romp* sound like?

   a. pot
   b. toe
   c. for

4. How many syllables are there in *romanticism*?

5. How many meanings are there for the word *rook*?

6. What is the past of *romp*?

7. Where can you find the meaning of *röntgen*?

8. What is the other spelling of *Romansch*?

9. You do not have space at the end of the line to write *roommate*.
   Where can you separate it?

   a. roo- mmate
   b. room- mate
   c. roomm- ate

10. In which sentence is *raise the roof* used correctly?

    a. He raised the roof when his boss told him he had to work on
       Sunday.
    b. After the storm, he raised the roof on the damaged house.

11. Who was Romulus?

12. What kind of information can you find in a dictionary? Make a list.

Yazid wants to find out about English classes. Listen to his conversation
with the school secretary. Write down the answers to his questions.

1. When/begin?

2. When/finish?

3. When/classes meet?

4. Registration date?

5. Tuition?

6. Course includes

    a. grammar?
    b. pronunciation?
    c. conversation?
    d. American literature?
    e. composition

7. Facilities include

    a. language lab?
    b. video?
    c. tape recorders?
    d. computers?

These are two ads for language schools in the United States. Compare the two schools with your partner. Which school would you go to? Why?

Useful language

Classes at Concord are small*er than* classes at International.

Classes at Concord aren't *as* large *as* classes at International.

International has classes in TOEFL preparation, *but* Concord doesn't.

Student A

Four language school owners are looking for students for their schools. The students need to decide which school is best.

Language School Owners

The people in the class are possible students for your school. There are three owners of other language schools. They also want students for their schools.

You must convince the possible students that your school is better than the other three. A representative from each group will come and talk to you. First, decide:

a. the name of your school
b. the number of weeks/months per course
c. the number of class hours a week
d. tuition
e. the number of students in a class
f. type of courses, e.g., TOEFL preparation
g. facilities at your school, e.g., language lab
h. anything else you think is important

STUDENT B: Turn to page 205.

1. Read this letter to the International Language School. Note the important features of a business letter.

46 Ventouri St.
Athens 15561
Greece

Dec. 28, 1986

International Language School
3015 S. Congress
Austin TX 78704

Dear Madam/Sir :

I am interested in studying English for two months in the United States and would like some information about your school.

I am twenty-four years old and am studying English at a language school in Athens. I work at an American company so I need to speak English well.

Could you please send me an application form? I would also like to know when classes begin, how long they last and how much the tuition is.

I look forward to hearing from you soon.

Sincerely,

(Mr.) Dimitris Sparis

2. Use this information to write a letter to the Concord School of English. (There are four paragraphs and ten sentences.)

kamishakuji 4-16-2 tokyo 145 may 14 1986 concord school of english 23 essex street concord new hampshire 03301 dear madam or sir one of the teachers at my school here in tokyo told me that your school has summer courses i am planning to come to the united states next summer and would like to take a short one-month course i am 18 years old and have been studying english for six years i am going to study english at the university i have never been to the us before and think a trip will help me improve my english could you send me a catalogue and application form i would also like information about new hampshire and other places nearby i hope to do some traveling when the course is over thank you in advance i look forward to your reply very truly yours mariko kobori

Write a letter to a language school. Ask for information about the school and give information about yourself. Remember to use the correct business letter format.

Unit Eighteen
IN THE NEWS

1. Read your horoscope. Does the near future look good or bad?

AQUARIUS (Jan. 20–Feb. 18)
This is the time to make some money. Look around for ways to invest. Don't be afraid. You could make big profits. Follow friends' advice.

PISCES (Feb. 19–March 20)
Someone has been keeping a secret. You'll find out what it is today. It could be important to your romantic life. Don't be shocked.

ARIES (March 21–April 19)
New problems at work. Boss makes many demands. Keep calm. Don't lose temper. It could be a test for better things to come.

TAURUS (April 20–May 20)
Travel and children are important in the near future. Think carefully before changing jobs. You meet wonderful people when you accept an invitation.

GEMINI (May 21–June 20)
Be careful with your money and possessions. You could lose them easily to the request of others. Don't be too friendly with strangers.

CANCER (June 21–July 21)
Arguments with friends and family are at the center of things. Don't take them too seriously. The problems will soon pass.

LEO (July 23–Aug. 22)
Love looks good but take your time. Getting serious too fast could lead to problems. Enjoy this period. It doesn't happen twice.

VIRGO (Aug. 23–Sept. 22)
Nothing exciting happening to you these days. Just keep working hard and be patient. Things are bound to change.

LIBRA (Sept. 23–Oct. 22)
A change in career is just around the corner. The money might not be as good, but the work will be far more interesting. Don't turn it down.

SCORPIO (Oct. 23–Nov. 21)
Don't be so interested in money. You ignore other good things. Look around for other interests. Make some new friends.

SAGITTARIUS (Nov. 22–Dec. 21)
Friends may ask your advice. Be careful in what you say. You could be blamed if things go wrong. Friends can easily become enemies.

CAPRICORN (Dec. 22–Jan. 19)
You need a vacation. You've been busy at work and at home. You get angry very easily. Go away to the mountains or the shore. The fresh air and peace and quiet will do you good.

2. Match each word in Column A with its meaning in Column B. Do 1 to 6, a to g first. (Number 3 has been done for you.)

	Column A		Column B
____	1. invest (Aquarius)	a.	don't be in a hurry
____	2. lose temper (Aries)	b.	get angry
_a_	3. be patient (Virgo)	c.	give money so that you can make more money
____	4. are bound to (Virgo)		
____	5. turn down (Libra)	d.	not pay attention to
____	6. ignore (Scorpio)	e.	will certainly happen
		f.	say "no"
____	7. big profits (Aquarius)	g.	a lot of money
____	8. secret (Pisces)	h.	something that is yours
____	9. shocked (Pisces)	i.	angry talk
____	10. possession (Gemini)	j.	beauty
____	11. argument (Cancer)	k.	very surprised
____	12. just around the corner (Libra)	l.	something that you do not tell anybody
____	13. enemies (Sagittarius)	m.	very near
		n.	people you hate

3. Write the horoscope sign next to the topics that the horoscopes mention. (Number 8 has been done for you.)

1. love/romance

2. career/work

3. family

4. friends

5. money

6. children

7. travel/vacation

8. new people   Taurus   Gemini   Scorpio

4. Discuss the answers to these questions with your partner.

1. Which horoscope has the best news?

2. Which horoscope has the worst news?

Imagine that one day you open up the newspaper and find your "dream" horoscope. It says just what you have always wanted for your future.

1. Make notes on these topics:
   a. money
   b. work
   c. travel
   d. romance
   e. family
   f. friends

2. Write your "dream" horoscope.

Eileen is going to tell her friend Martha how to make a paper fortune teller. This is a game that predicts the future.

Listen to the conversation. Follow the illustrations below.

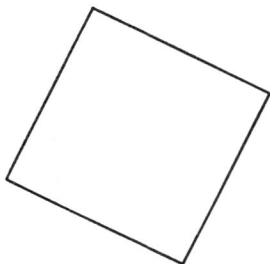
1.

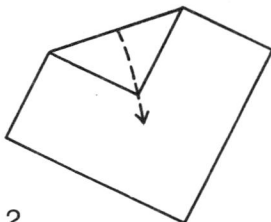
2.

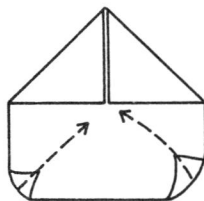
3.

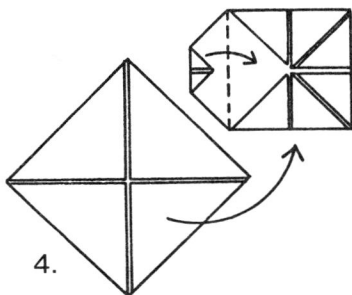
4.

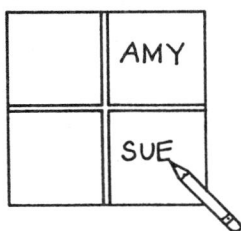
5.

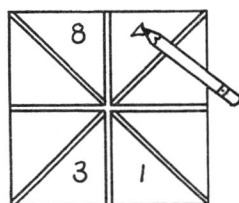
6.

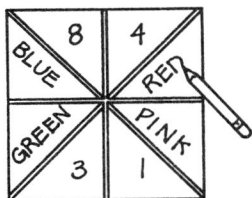
7.

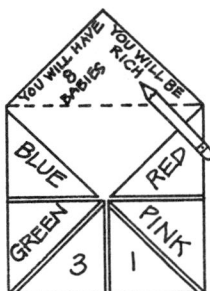
8.

9.

Tell another person how to make a paper fortune teller. Discuss the instructions with your partner. Look at the pictures and use these words to help you:

fold   middle   line
turn over   corner   side
              square
              triangle

Make a fortune teller. Write four names, four numbers, four colors, and eight predictions. Lift the four boxes with the names on them and put your two thumbs and two index fingers under them. Your partner chooses first a name, then a number (or color), then a color (or number). For the first two choices, move your thumbs and fingers together and apart while you spell the word. For the last choice, lift the piece of paper and read the fortune to your partner. Then play the game with other people in the class. Make a list with everyone's name. Write the predictions next to the names.

When do you think these things will happen? Discuss the answers with your partner. Then compare your predictions with the rest of the class.

1. When will people start taking vacations on the moon?
2. When will people start carrying televisions in their pockets?
3. When will Americans elect a woman for president?
4. When will scientists find a cure for cancer?
5. When will an American soccer team win the World Cup?
6. When will a cup of coffee cost $5 (or the equivalent in your country)?
7. When will people stop fighting wars?

Useful language

I think people will _____ by 1995.
                              in (the next) 10 years.

People will probably _____ before the turn of the century.

I don't think people will ever _____ .

ROUND THREE

Unit Nineteen
PEOPLE

1. Look at the picture. What cartoon characters are in the picture? Read the caption underneath the picture. Answer the questions.

1. When did Walt Disney make Donald Duck?

2. What animals were in the movie "Bambi"?

©**Walt Disney Productions**

Cartoon characters, such as Mickey Mouse, Donald Duck and Pinocchio, made Walt Disney known to people throughout the world. Mickey Mouse first appeared in a short cartoon in 1928. Donald Duck made his first appearance in 1934. Other characters created by Disney include Pinocchio and Snow White and the Seven Dwarfs.

2. Read the text. Answer the questions.

1. Where was Walt Disney born?

2. How old was he when he went to Los Angeles?

3. What cartoon character first made Walt Disney famous?

DISNEY, WALT (1901–1966) was one of the most famous motion-picture producers in history. Disney first became known in the 1920s and 1930s for creating such cartoon film characters as Mickey Mouse and Donald
5 Duck. He later produced feature-length cartoon films, movies about wild animals in their natural surroundings, and films starring human actors. . . .

Early Life. Walter Elias Disney was born in Chicago. His family moved to Missouri when he was a child, and
10 Disney spent much of his boyhood on a farm near Marceline. At the age of 16, Disney studied art in Chicago. In 1920, he joined the Kansas City Film Ad Company, where he helped make crude cartoon advertisements to be shown in movie theaters.

15 *The First Disney Cartoons.* In 1923, Disney moved to Los Angeles to become a filmmaker. After he failed to find work, he returned to drawing movie cartoons. He set up his first studio in back of a real estate office. For several years, Disney struggled just to pay his expenses.
20 He finally gained success* in 1928, when he released the first short Mickey Mouse cartoons. †

*Gained success: was successful.
† He released the first short Mickey Mouse cartoons: people could see Mickey Mouse cartoons at movie theaters.

3. What do these words refer to?

  1. he (line 5)

  2. their (line 6)

  3. his (line 9)

  4. where (line 13)

4. Choose the correct answer.

  1. *create* (line 3) means

    a. make
    b. buy

  2. *wild* (line 6) means

    a. animals like dogs and cats
    b. animals like lions and elephants

3. *boyhood* (line 10) means

    a. until about the age of 12
    b. until about the age of 30

4. *struggled* (line 19) means

    a. had fights with people
    b. had a difficult time

5. Fill in the chart with facts about the life of Walt Disney.

Date	Event	Place
_____	Disney was born.	_____
XXXX	Disney and his family moved.	_____
1917	Disney _____	_____
1920	Disney _____	XXXXXXXXXXXXXX
_____	Disney _____	Los Angeles
1928	Disney _____	Los Angeles
1966	Disney _____	XXXXXXXXXXXXXX

Turn to page 132. You have information about one famous person and your partner has information about another. Ask your partner about this person. Write down the answers and guess who he or she is.

Useful language

Where _____ from?

Where| _____ born?

When |

Where| _____ die?

When |

What type of work _____ do?

Why _____ famous?

Student A

1. Answer your partner's questions. Do not say the name of the famous person.
(Abraham Lincoln)

Nationality: American
Date of Birth: Feb. 12, 1809
Date of Death: April 15, 1865
Reason for being famous:
   President of the United States
   during the American Civil War
   (1861–1865)

Occupation: Lawyer/Politician
Place of Birth: Kentucky
Place of Death: Washington, D.C.

2. Ask your partner questions. Write down the answers. Guess the name of the famous person.

Nationality:
Date of Birth:
Date of Death:
Reason for being famous:

Occupation:
Place of Birth:
Place of Death:

Name: _____

STUDENT B: Turn to page 206.

1. Read this paragraph about Walt Disney.

   Walt Disney, the American film producer, was born in Chicago in 1901. He was famous for creating well-known cartoon characters such as Donald Duck and Mickey Mouse. He also built Disneyland, the famous amusement park in California. He died in 1966 in Switzerland.

2. Write a paragraph about Abraham Lincoln or Charlie Chaplin.

Listen to the game show. Guess who the famous person is.

Play The Fame Game. In groups choose the names of two or three famous people. (They should not be alive.) Write down the information that your group will tell the other groups about each person. (Remember! Don't make it too easy!) The other groups can ask you five questions. Answer only with "yes" or "no." If one of the groups guesses the name of a famous person, that group gets a point. If nobody can guess, then your group gets a point. The group that has the most points at the end of the game will be the winner.

Useful language

Was this person a woman?

Was this person from _____ ?

Did this person live in the _____ century?

Did this person write music?

Was this person a(n) (artist, politician, entertainer)?

1. Read this paragraph about the life of Indira Gandhi.

   Indira Gandhi, one of the great woman leaders of the 20th century, was born in Uttar Pradesh, India. Her father, Jawaharlal Nehru, was the first prime minister of India. She was very close to him and so was always interested in politics. *When* she finished her studies in England, she returned to India and became involved in the fight for India's independence from Great Britain. India became independent in 1948. She became president of her father's party, the Congress Party, *in* 1959, and five years *later* she became Minister of Information and Broadcasting. *After* the death of Prime Minister Shastri in 1966, she became prime minister of India. Her husband's name was Ferez Gandhi. She lost reelection in 1977, but became prime minister again in 1980. She was killed *on* October 31, 1984, in New Delhi. She had two sons.

2. Cross out the three sentences that do not belong in the paragraph.

3. Write a paragraph about the life of a famous person from your country.

Unit Twenty
AT HOME

1. Look at the medicine labels below and on the following page. Which medicine should you take if:

   a. you have a cough?
   b. your eyes are bothering you?
   c. you have a headache?

Label 1

NDC 12843-101-20

Genuine

BAYER
ASPIRIN ®

Micro-Thin Coating

Fast Pain Relief of headache, muscular aches and pains, the aches and fever due to colds and flu, and the temporary relief of minor arthritis pain.

200 TABLETS-325 MG. (5 GRS.) EACH

12093 C5

Use Only If Printed Seal Under Cap is Intact.

Adult Dose: 1 or 2 tablets with water every 4 hours, up to 12 a day.

WARNINGS: Consult a physician before giving this medicine to children, including teenagers, with chicken pox or flu. Keep this and all drugs out of the reach of children. In case of accidental overdose, seek professional assistance or contact a poison control center immediately. As with any drug, if you are pregnant or nursing a baby, seek the advice of a health professional before using this product. See important directions in leaflet, including use in arthritis and rheumatism.

EXP10-87
50765

The Bayer Company, Glenbrook Laboratories Div. of Sterling Drug Inc. New York, N.Y. 10016

12004 C5

Label 2

mediquell
CHEWY COUGH SQUARES

Relieves coughs due to colds, flu, bronchial irritation

Mediquell is a pleasant tasting cough medicine concentrated into soft, chewable squares. Mediquell contains the maximum allowable dose of dextromethorphan, a safe and effective cough suppressant, so each dose relieves coughs for up to 8 hours. Mediquell is non-narcotic and is safe for children and adults.

DIRECTIONS FOR USE: Chew and swallow Mediquell according to the following dose indications:

Adult Dose: 12 years and over —2 squares
Child Dose: 6-12 years — 1 square
2-6 years — ½ square
Under 2 years: use only as directed by a physician
Repeat every 6 to 8 hours as needed. Do not exceed 4 doses per day.

WARNINGS: Do not use if cough persists for more than one week or if high fever is present since these may indicate the presence of a serious condition. As with any drug, if you are pregnant or nursing a baby, seek the advice of a health professional before using this product.
Do not take this product for persistent or chronic cough such as occurs with smoking, asthma or emphysema or where cough is accompanied by excessive secretions except under the advice and supervision of a physician. Keep this and all medicines out of the reach of children.

ACTIVE INGREDIENT: Each square contains — Dextromethorphan Hydrobromide 15 mg.
Store at room temperature.

PATENT PENDING

WARNER-LAMBERT COMPANY • MORRIS PLAINS, NJ 07950

Label 3

sterile ● eye drops
Murine.®
Regular Clear Formula

for irritated eyes

cleansing·refreshing·soothing

0.5 FL. OZ.

Murine Regular Formula is a non-staining, clear solution formulated to more closely match the natural fluid of the eye for gentle, soothing relief from minor irritation. The product is sterile and contains scientifically blended and clinically tested ingredients.

When To Use: Morning and night or whenever desired to cleanse or refresh the eyes and to relieve minor irritation due to smog, sun glare, wind, dust, wearing contact lenses and overuse of the eyes in reading, driving, TV and close work. If _faster_ removal of redness is desired use Murine Plus also available at your store.

Directions: Tilt head back, squeeze two or three drops into each eye several times a day or as directed by physician.

Warnings: Do not touch bottle tip to any surface since this may contaminate solution. If irritation persists or increases, discontinue use and consult physician. Remove contact lenses before using. KEEP THIS AND ALL OTHER MEDICINES OUT OF REACH OF CHILDREN. Keep container tightly closed.

3

N 0074-557405

The Murine Company, Division Abbott Laboratories, North Chicago, Ill. 60064 Made in U.S.A.
91-4213/3R2 List 5574

2. Choose the correct answer.

1. *Physician* (Labels 1, 2, 3) means

   a. Doctor
   b. Lawyer
   c. Mechanic

2. *Keep . . . out of the reach of children* (Labels 1, 2, 3) means

   a. Give the medicine to children after you ask the doctor
   b. Do not put medicine in a place where children can get it easily
   c. Do not tell children why you are giving them the medicine

3. *Up to* (Labels 1, 2) means

   a. More than
   b. Less than
   c. Not more than

4. *Dose* (Labels 1, 2) means

   a. How much medicine you should buy
   b. How much medicine you should take
   c. How much medicine you should pay for

5. *In case of accidental overdose* (Label 1) means

   a. If someone buys the wrong medicine
   b. If someone forgets to take the medicine
   c. If someone takes too much medicine

6. *Consult* (Labels 1, 3) and *Seek the advice* (Label 2) mean

   a. Drive to
   b. Pay
   c. Talk to

7. *Tilt back* (Label 3) means

a.

b.

c.

3. Fill in the chart with the correct information.

	Bayer	Mediquell	Murine
How often you should take it			
How much you should take at one time			
How much a 3-year-old child should take at one time	✕		✕
Where you should keep the medicine			
What you should do if you take too much medicine		✕	✕

Listen to the conversation. Fill in the form on the following page.

New Patient — Medical Information

Name: *Michelle Santini*　　　　Sex: M F　　　　Age:

Height:　　　　　　　　　　　　Weight:

Reason for Visit: *General physical exam (for work)*

Smoke?

Drink?

Exercise?

	NO	YES	Details
Recent Medical History			
any colds?			
any sore throats?			
any bad coughs?			
the flu?			
any stomachaches?			
any headaches?			
any earaches?			
any toothaches?			
any backaches?			
any pains in chest?			
any pains in shoulder?			
any pains in legs?			
Past Medical History			
a broken leg?			
a sprained ankle?			
a broken arm?			

Imagine that you are a doctor and your partner is your patient. Ask questions about his or her health. Fill in the form on the following page.

Useful language

Have you had | any | pains in your chest | recently?
           | a | bad cough |
           | the | flu |

    Yes, I have. In fact I had _____ last week.

    Yeah, I had a terrible _____ the other day.

    Yes, I've had many _____ | the past few weeks.
                                  | recently.
    No, I haven't.

Have you ever | had a broken _____ ?

               | broken your _____ ?

    Yes, I have. I broke my arm once when I was 6.
    Yes. When I was 6, I fell down and broke my arm.

Do you smoke?
    Yes, | I do.   No, | never.
         | all the time. | not much.
         | every day.

How often do you _____ ?
    Every day.
    Once in a while.
    Almost never.

New Patient — Medical Information

Name: Sex: M   F   Age:

Height: Weight:

Reason for Visit:
Smoke?
Drink?
Exercise?

	NO	YES	Details
Recent Medical History			
any colds?			
any sore throats?			
any bad coughs?			
the flu?			
any stomachaches?			
any headaches?			
any earaches?			
any toothaches?			
any backaches?			
any pains in chest?			
any pains in shoulder?			
any pains in legs?			
Past Medical History			
a broken leg?			
a sprained ankle?			
a broken arm?			

Look at the sign. What do you think some of the "simple rules" are?

1. Discuss it with your partner.

2. Make a list and fill in the sign.

STAY HEALTHY

Follow these simple rules and your visits to the
doctor will be few and far between.

-
-
-
-
-

People do different things when they are not feeling well. What do you do
when you have a headache or stomachache?

1. Put a check (✓) next to the remedy you use. Add your own remedies if
they are not on the list.

2. Ask the other people in your group about their remedies. Write their
initials in the appropriate columns.

	Headache	Stomachache	Earache	Toothache	Sore Throat	Cold	Flu	Backache
drink hot milk								
drink hot tea								
drink lots of liquids								
drink coffee								
drink whisky or brandy								
eat yogurt								
take an aspirin								
take medicine								
gargle								
lie down								
lie on your stomach								
stay in bed								
take a hot bath or shower								
get a massage								

other remedies

143

Did you learn any interesting remedies? Do members of your family (for example, your grandparents or parents) use interesting remedies not on the list? Tell the others in your class.

YOUR HEALTH

by Dr. Rubin

Dear Dr. Rubin,
I'm 60 pounds overweight and just about at the end of my rope. I've tried just about every diet there is, but every time I lose weight I seem to gain more back. Please help me. I feel terrible and look worse.

Esther Mills

Dear Esther,
Exercise and healthy eating are the only answers. No more crazy diets! Join a health club. Start swimming a few times a week. Take long walks. Stop thinking about *not* eating. Eat! Eat healthy foods—fruit and vegetables and fish—and you'll find you won't want all that cake and ice cream you probably now dream about.
Good luck and happy eating!

Dr. R.

1. Read these two letters to Dr. Rubin.

Dear Dr. Rubin,
I'm sixteen years old and have a terrible skin problem. My face is full of pimples. Everyone looks at me all the time. What can I do?

Peggy Newman

Dear Dr. Rubin,
I've had back problems for several months now and don't know what to do. One doctor I went to told me I shouldn't lift heavy things. But I am a construction worker. How can I not lift heavy things? It's my work and my life. Do you have any advice? Quitting my job is no solution.

Jack MacDonald

2. Write Dr. Rubin's reply to one of the letters.

3. a. Write a short letter to another student about a problem (or an imaginary problem) you have. He or she will send you a reply with some advice.

b. Read the letter you receive. Write a reply and give some advice.

Unit Twenty-One
AT HOME

1. Read the washing machine instructions on page 146. Put the pictures in the correct order.

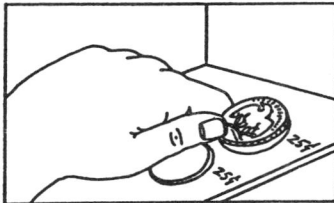

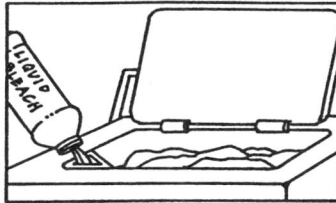

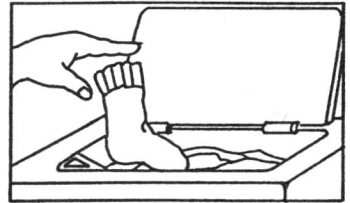

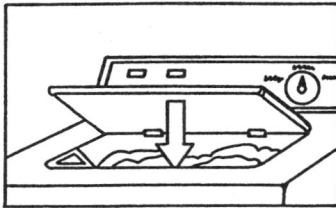

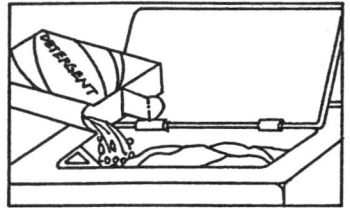

HOT WASH FOR • COLORFAST COTTONS
WARM WASH FOR • REGULAR PERMANENT PRESS
COLD WASH FOR • SPECIAL FABRICS

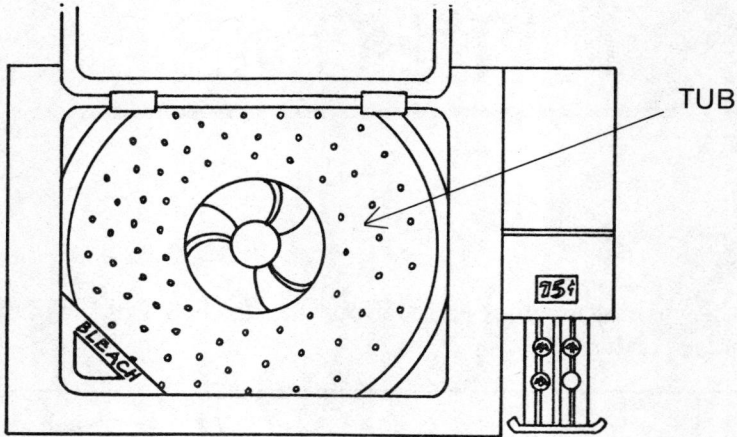

TUB

TO OPERATE

1. PLACE SORTED CLOTHES IN TUB. DO NOT PACK.
2. ADD MEASURED DETERGENT.
3. SELECT DESIRED WATER TEMPERATURE (AND WASH/SPIN—
   IF AVAILABLE).
4. POUR MEASURED AMOUNT OF DILUTED BLEACH INTO BLEACH
   DISPENSER, IF DESIRED. MAXIMUM RECOMMENDED AMOUNT
   IS 1-1/4 CUPS.
5. CLOSE LID. INSERT COINS IN SLIDE OR SLOTS. SLIDE MUST BE
   MOVED IN AND OUT SLOWLY TO START WASHER PROPERLY.
   LID MUST BE CLOSED FOR WASHER TO OPERATE.
6. LEAVE LID OPEN AFTER REMOVING CLOTHES.

IMPORTANT

FOR PERSONAL SAFETY—BE SURE ALL PARTS OF WASHER
HAVE STOPPED MOVING COMPLETELY BEFORE REACHING
INTO THE WASHER OR LOADING, ADDING OR UNLOADING
CLOTHES. TO STOP MACHINE, RAISE LID TO FULLY OPEN
POSITION AND WAIT FOR MOVING PARTS TO STOP.

WASHER OPERATES ONLY WHEN LID IS CLOSED

G-145-0

2. Put a T if the statement is true and an F if the statement is false.

1. _____ Put in as many clothes as you want.

2. _____ Measure how much detergent you need and then put it in the machine.

3. _____ Do not use more than 2 cups of bleach.

4. _____ This machine only starts when the lid is closed.

5. _____ When the machine has stopped, take out your clothes and close the lid.

Joan Henderson's washing machine isn't working. She calls three repair shops. Fill in the chart with the information she gets.

	GENERAL REPAIR	ABE APPLIANCES	C & R REPAIRS
a. Does the shop repair washing machines?			
b. How much does the shop charge an hour?			
c. Are parts additional?			
d. When is the earliest someone from the shop can come?			
e. What is the name of the repairman?			

With some kinds of cameras it is possible to take a picture and see it in less than 60 seconds. Look at the pictures and see how to work this type of camera. Discuss how to use it with your partner. Make notes. Use these words to help you:

film   tear off
viewfinder   peel off

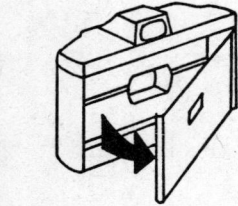

1.

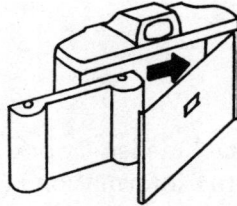

2.

3.

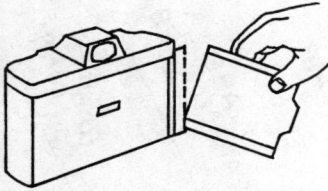

4.

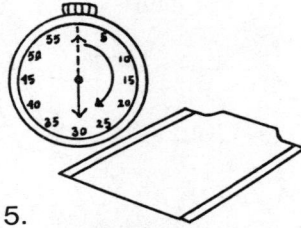

5.

6.

1. Read this paragraph on how to use a coin-operated washing machine.

First, put the clothes in the machine. Then, add the detergent and choose the water temperature you want. After that, pour in the bleach, if you're going to use any. Finally, close the lid and insert your money. Then the machine will start.

2. Use your notes to write a paragraph on how to use an instamatic (automatic) camera. Use these words to help you:

first   after that
then   finally

1. Your partner is going to describe two or three of these objects. Ask questions about the objects. Point to the ones that you think he or she is describing.

2. Describe two or three of the objects to your partner. He or she has to guess what you are describing. Describe:

a. the material
b. the size
c. the color
d. its function
e. the cost

Useful language

What's the object made of?

    It's made of _____ .

How big is _____ ?
    tall
    high
    long
    It's 5 inches by 2 feet.
    It's 10 inches high.
                 long.
                 wide.

What's the object used for?
    It's used   for taking pictures.
                 to take pictures.

1. Read this description of a washing machine.

    A washing machine is used for washing clothes. It's made of metal and plastic and can come in many sizes and colors. It costs from $300 to $650.

2. Write descriptions for two of the objects on page 149.

Unit Twenty-Two
AT WORK

1. Look at the help wanted ads on page 152. Find the abbreviations for these words. Numbers 6 and 11 have been done for you.

1. minimum	_____	11. excellent	<u>excl</u>	<u>exc</u>
2. company	_____	12. between	_____	_____
3. experienced*	_____	13. receptionist	_____	
4. years	_____	14. office	_____	
5. benefits†	_____	15. position¶	_____	
6. thousand	<u>K</u>	16. with	_____	
7. manager	_____	17. hours per week	_____	
8. references‡	_____	18. assistant	_____	
9. full time§	_____	19. words per minute	_____	
10. part time	_____	20. executive	_____	

* Experienced: have done this sort of work before
† Benefits: for example, extra money for health insurance
‡ References: people who know you and can say that you will do a good job
§ Full time: around 40 hours a week
¶ Position: job

2. Answer the questions.

   1. Which jobs require knowledge of a foreign language?

     a.

     b.

     c.

2. Which ads give the salary?

    a.

    b.

    c.

3. Which jobs have an age requirement?

    a.

    b.

4. Which ads say that the people will train you to do the job?

    a.

    b.

    c.

5. Which jobs require typing skills?

    a.

    b.

    c.

6. Which jobs require a good speaking voice on the telephone?

    a.   c.

    b.   d.

7. Which jobs are *or* can be part time?

    a.   c.   e.

    b.   d.

8. For which jobs must you send a résumé?

    a.   c.

    b.   d.

9. Which ads tell you what time to telephone?

    a.

    b.

    c.

10. Which ads tell you to go to the place and apply for the job?

    a.

    b.

3. What number should these people call, or to whom should they write?

1. Diane has been a secretary for 3-1/2 years. She types 55 w.p.m.

2. Allen has just finished university. He has good grades and has not chosen a career yet.

3. Nick is 23 years old and has 2 years' experience as a chauffeur.

4. Anne's children are all in school now, and she wants to get a job. She has no experience and only wants to work part time.

4. Do you want to apply for any of these jobs? Which one(s)?

Abbreviations are often used in want ads to save space.

1. Read this unabbreviated ad for the auto rental manager on page 152.

The person must be bilingual (English/Spanish) and experienced. He or she will get a company car, health benefits, and a salary and commission of over $30,000. If interested, please call (718) 426-5454.

2. Write out these ads in complete sentences.

1.   Supermkt. needs exp. cashiers   25 yrs or older   5 days, 11–7
       Call (512) 693-4224

2.   COMPUTER PROGRAMMER for lg electronic co
       2 yrs exp   40 hrs/wk $35,000/yr
       Send résumé to: Victoria Haines, 729 Park Ave. NY NY 10014

3.   PROJECT MGR.
       Oil co. operating in Kuwait seeks civil egr. with exp on
       construction sites. Knowl Arabic nec   9 mos/yr $70K+ exc
       bnfts.   Send résumé to: P.O. Box 727 Dallas TX 75220

Al Martinez, the owner and manager of the Grande Dining Restaurant, interviews three different people to work in his restaurant. Listen to the interviews. Fill in the chart and decide who should get the job.

	Eleanor Lance		Lisa Alder	
Previous Experience Name of business Length of time	Marriott Inn	Olympia Diner	Tom's Restaurant	Alder's Supermarket
Type of Work Wanted Full time	☐		☐	
Part time	☐		☐	
Available Day	☐		☐	
Evening	☐		☐	
Transportation				
Starting Date				

Vince Walker saw the ad for an accountant on page 152. He called to make an appointment and spoke to Ms. Carpenter.

1. Read Ms. Carpenter's part of the conversation.

2. Discuss with your partner what Vince said. Complete the conversation.

3. Repeat the conversation with your partner.

Vince: Hello. May I _____

Ms. Carpenter: Speaking.

Vince: Hello. My name _____

                  I'm calling _____

Ms. Carpenter: Oh. You mean the one that was in Saturday's paper.

Vince:	Yes. Is it _____
Ms. Carpenter:	Yes, it is. Do you have any experience?
Vince:	Yes _____
	I was wondering if I could _____
Ms. Carpenter:	Yes, certainly. When would be the best time for you?
Vince:	Could I _____
Ms. Carpenter:	I'm afraid I have another appointment at that time.
Vince:	How about _____
Ms. Carpenter:	That would be fine.
Vince:	Can you tell me _____
Ms. Carpenter:	It's 7318 Holland Avenue, and my office is on the 4th floor.
Vince:	Fine. Thank you. I'll see _____
Ms. Carpenter:	I'm looking forward to it. Good-bye.
Vince:	_____

4. Imagine that you have seen an ad for a job you would like. Your partner is the employer. Call up and set up an appointment. Try not to look at the conversation between Vince and Ms. Carpenter.

What type of work do you do? Or, what type of work do you hope to do when you finish school?

What skills and/or qualifications do you need for this type of work?

1. Make a list under "Requirements."

Job:

Requirements

	NAMES					

2. Find out if other people in your group could do this type of work. Ask them about each of your requirements. Put a check (✓) if the answer is *yes* and an ✕ if the answer is *no*. Find out who would be the most qualified person in your group to do this sort of work.

Useful language

Can you _____ ?
    Yes, I can.
    No, I can't.
    No, I'm afraid not.

Have you ever _____ ?

Do you know _____ ?

Do you know how to _____ ?
    Yes, I do.
    No, I don't.
    No, I'm afraid I don't.
    Not very well, I'm afraid.

Brian Casey is applying for the job as a paralegal assistant in the ad on page 152.

1. Read his letter. In which paragraph does he

    a. give personal information?
    b. give his reason for writing?
    c. say where Ms. Baker can contact him?

---

863 Union St.
Brooklyn, NY 11215
July 26, 1986

Ms. Virginia Baker
Herrick Feinstein
2 Park Avenue
New York, NY 10016

Dear Ms. Baker:

I would like to apply for the job as a paralegal worker which was advertised in Saturday's New York Times.

As you can see from the enclosed résumé, I graduated from Brooklyn College two months ago. I majored in English and had very good grades. I might apply to law school in a few years, and a job at Herrick Feinstein would be a good opportunity to get some experience in a law office.

Please contact me at the above address or telephone me at (718) 221-3936. You can reach me anytime before noon.

I look forward to your reply.

Sincerely,

Brian Casey

Brian Casey

---

2. Write a letter and apply for a job advertised on page 152 or an imaginary job you would like to have.

Unit Twenty-Three
ENTERTAINMENT

1. Look at the movie reviews. Which film

a. is a funny police story?
b. has music
c. is about spies?
d. is about war?

Movies

Beverly Hills Cop ★★★ (R) Eddie Murphy is very, very funny as Axel Foley, a Detroit detective who goes to Southern California to solve the murder of an old pal. Director Martin Brest keeps the whole thing moving at a brisk clip, and the frequent high moments distract us from reflecting on the fact that, basically, it's just another formulaic police thriller. — *R.L.*

The Killing Fields ★★★★ (R) First-time director Roland Joffe's spectacular adaptation of New York Times correspondent Sydney Schanberg's memoir about his relationship with his Cambodian translator, Dith Pran, during the brutal rise of the Khmer Rouge. A harrowing antiwar epic with an emotional resonance and a depth of texture that puts it in the company of the best films of the decade. A must. — *R.L.*

The Falcon and the Snowman ★★★ (R) John Schlesinger's provocative and fascinating account of two young American spies is a film — like *Another Country* — that reduces the age of treason. Its strength lies in the way it captures the confusion and tangled emotions of youth rather than indulging in pat explanations. Sean Penn and Tim Hutton are exceptional as the two traitors who sell CIA secrets to the KGB. — *D.R.*

Stop Making Sense ★★★ (No MPAA rating.) A film of Talking Heads' 1983 tour, directed by Jonathan Demme, whose previous films include *Melvin and Howard.* It's a seamless, efficient movie, but one lacking the sweat and jaggedness of great rock-and-roll. This is a rock movie for people who don't go to rock concerts. — *K.T.*

Ratings: ★★★★ Excellent   ★★★ Good   ★★ Fair   ★ Poor
Reviewers: D.R.—Desmond Ryan   R.L.—Rick Lyman   K.T.—Ken Tucker

2. Fill in the chart.

	Setting	Rating	Actors	Director
Beverly Hills Cop				
The Falcon and the Snowman	✕			
The Killing Fields			✕	
Stop Making Sense	✕		✕	

****Excellent   ***Good   **Fair   *Poor

3. Fill in these summaries. Choose the correct answers.

1. *Beverly Hills Cop* is about a detective from _____ who goes
   a. California
   b. Detroit

   to _____ because he wants to find the _____
   a. California   a. doctor
   b. Detroit   b. killer

   of an old _____ .
   a. friend
   b. teacher

2. *The Falcon and the Snowman* is about _____ young
   a. two
   b. three

   Americans who sell secret information to the _____
   a. CIA
   b. KGB

   and about _____ they do it.
   a. why
   b. when

3. *The Killing Fields* is about a man who works for a famous American

_____ and _____ ,   the man who translated
a. newspaper   a. Dith Pran
b. TV station   b. Sydney Schanberg

for the reporter in _____ at the time of the war there.
                          a. New York
                          b. Cambodia

4. *Stop Making Sense* is a film about the trip the rock group

_____   made around the United States
a. Melvin and Howard
b. Talking Heads

in _____ . It is a film for people who like films
     a. 1983
     b. 1985

_____ .

a. with lots of rock music
b. about the lives of rock musicians

4. Which film would you like to see? Why?

Listen to the movie reviews. Fill in the chart.

	Rating	Type of Story
Wronged		
When You Find Love		
The Kid Rides Again		

****Excellent   ***Good   **Fair   *Poor

Find out what films people in your group have seen recently. Fill in the chart below.

Name of Classmate	Name of Film	Story	Actors	Classmate's Opinion	Your Opinion (If you've seen the film)

Useful language

What film have you seen recently?
When did you see it?

What did you think of it?
    I really liked it.   So did I.
                                     I did too.
    It was okay.
    I couldn't stand it. Neither could I.
                                     I couldn't either.

Did you like it?
    Yes, I thought it was | great.
                              | fantastic.
                              | very good.

    No, I thought it was | awful.
                              | terrible.

This paragraph about the film, *Wronged*, has no grammar mistakes. However, it is not a good paragraph.

1. Read the paragraph and discuss what is wrong with it with your partner.

I saw the film *Wronged* last week. *Wronged* was a true story. *Wronged* was about a man. The man's name was Arthur Thompson. Thompson went to jail for fifteen years for murder. Thompson did not commit the murder. *Wronged* starred Henry Michaelson and Joanne Seymour. Henry Michaelson and Joanne Seymour played husband and wife in *Wronged*. Henry Michaelson and Joanne Seymour were both very good. I enjoyed *Wronged* very much. The story was sad. The story was interesting. The acting was very good.

2. Write the paragraph again and try to improve it.

3. Write a description of a film you have seen recently. Say what it was about, who was in it, whether or not you liked it, and why.

1. Make a list of things to do in your town.

Movies	Restaurants	Interesting places (Museums, historical sites, zoos, etc.)	Other places (Discos, concerts, sporting events)

2. Make plans to meet with other classmates on the weekend. Talk about what to do and where and what time to meet.

Useful language

What	about going to see _____ (instead)?
How	

Why don't we	go and see _____ (instead)?
Let's	

That sounds	good.
	like fun.

I'm not crazy about	that restaurant.
	going to that restaurant.

I don't feel like going to that restaurant.

Where	should we meet?
What time	

1. Read this note.

> Sept. 3rd
>
> Dear Jose,
>   Yoshi, Ali and I are going to have dinner at Conrad's. That's on Liberty Ave. We're going to meet outside the restaurant at 7 P.M.
>   Hope you'll join us.
>
>   Irene

2. Write a note to a classmate who is absent or who is in another group. Say what your group's plans are, and ask him or her to join you.

Unit Twenty-Four
GETTING SOMEWHERE

1. Which of these instructions is *not* important for good driving?

1. Slow down when you want to turn left or right.

2. Stop at red lights.

3. Don't drive too near the other cars on the road.

4. Use your blinkers (left or right) when you want to pass another car.

5. Don't eat too much before you start.

2. Read "Keeping a Space Cushion" on page 166. Which of the instructions above is the main topic of the text?

3. Find the words in the text with these meanings. The first letter of each word is written.

1. near	c _____	
2. in front	a _____	
3. place	s _____	
4. wet	s _____	
5. space	r _____	
6. fast	h _____	s _____

KEEPING A SPACE CUSHION

If another driver makes a mistake, you need time to react. The only way to be sure you'll have enough time is to leave plenty of space between you and the cars around you. Try to keep a cushion of space on all sides of you.

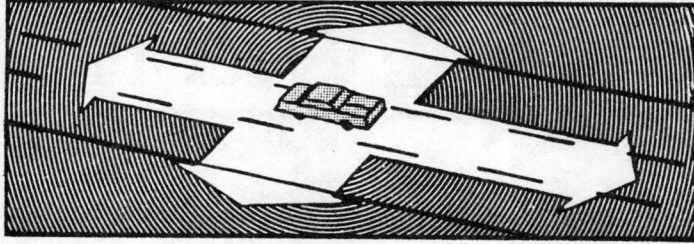

Keeping A Cushion Ahead

5   If you're following too closely and the car ahead stops or slows down suddenly, you may not be able to stop in time. How can you tell if you are far enough back? Use the two-second following rule.

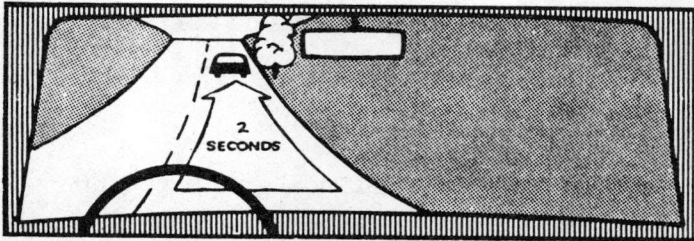

When the rear bumper of the car ahead passes a shadow or a
10   pavement marking, start counting the seconds it takes you to reach the same spot on the road. Count "one-second-one, two-seconds-two." If you pass the shadow or pavement marking before you finish, then you are following too closely.

In some situations you need an extra cushion. Allow a longer
15   following distance when:
- Traveling on slippery roads.
- Following motorcycles. If the motorcycle should fall, you'll need extra distance to avoid the rider. The chances of a fall are greatest on wet roads, metal surfaces, such as bridge gratings
20   or streetcar tracks, and gravel.
- The driver behind you wants to pass. Maintain a steady speed while being passed. Allow room in front of your car to help the drivers pass.
- Following drivers whose rear view is blocked. The drivers of
25   trucks, buses, vans or cars pulling campers or trailers can't see you very well. They could slow down suddenly without knowing you are behind them.
- Carrying a heavy load or pulling a trailer. The extra weight increases your braking distance.
30   - Driving at a high speed.

4. Choose the correct answer.

1. "you need time to react" (line 1) means

    a. you need time to do something
    b. you need time to start

2. "the rear bumper" (line 9) means

    a. the front of the car
    b. the back of the car

3. "the same spot on the road" (line 11) means

    a. the shadow or pavement marking
    b. the car in front of you

4. "to avoid the rider" (line 18) means

    a. not to hit the person on the motorcycle
    b. to say something to the person on the motorcycle

5. "Maintain a steady speed" (line 21) means

    a. go at a faster speed
    b. do not change speed

6. "rear view is blocked" (line 24) means

    a. (the driver) can see out of the back window of the car
    b. (the driver) cannot see out of the back window of the car

7. "a heavy load" (line 28) means

    a. the car weighs a lot
    b. the car is carrying things that weigh a lot

5. Answer the questions. Number 1 has been done for you.

1. The text says "you need time to react" (line 1). What do you need time to react to? *You need time to react to a mistake by another driver.*

2. The text says "The only way to be sure you'll have enough time" (lines 1 and 2). What will you want to have enough time to do?

3. The text says "When the rear bumper of the car ahead passes a shadow" (line 9). What will it be a shadow of?

4. The text says "If you pass the shadow or pavement marking before you finish" (lines 12 and 13). What should you finish doing?

5. The text says "then you are following too closely" (line 13). What are you following too closely?

6. Put a check (✓) if the text has this information.

1. The text tells you why it is important not to be too close to other cars.

2. The text tells you what to do if you are too close to other cars.

3. The text tells you how to check that you are not too close to other cars.

4. The text tells you when you need extra space between your car and the other cars.

5. The text tells you why it is important to always drive slowly.

Memory Quiz

1. Study the pictures for 1 minute. Write down 10 questions to ask your partner about them. (What? Where? How many?)

2. Close your book. Ask your partner your questions. Answer his or her questions. Who remembers more?

One of the people who witnessed the accident is telling a policewoman how it happened. However, he has made some mistakes. Listen to his account. Write down the 10 statements that are wrong.

The policewoman wrote up her report after she talked to the witnesses and drivers.

1. Read these sentences from her report.

   a. The driver of the car, Dave Walters, was going up 13th Street at the speed limit of 25 m.p.h.

   b. A truck was coming from the opposite direction and also stopped at the stop sign.

   c. The accident took place at 2 PM yesterday afternoon.

   d. He stopped at the stop sign.

   e. Two vehicles were involved.

   f. She ran right in front of the car.

   g. The car had about $500 worth of damage.

   h. They both started to go across Thompson Street, but just at that moment a child ran into the street after a ball.

   i. The damage to the truck, however, was minimal.

   j. Walters had to go quickly to his left in order not to hit her.

   k. Nobody was injured.

   l. That's when he ran into the truck.

2. Write the sentences in the correct order in the police report form.

ACCIDENT REPORT FORM

Officer: Catherine Stevens
Date of Accident: 3/30/8__   Time: 2 PM
Location of Accident: 13th & Thompson

Report _____

_____

_____

                                        Nobody was injured.

                    Signature _Catherine Stevens_

In groups of three role-play the scene between the police officer and the two drivers involved in the accident.

1. When you are the police officer, ask the drivers their names, addresses, and occupations. Ask to see their driver's licenses, and get details about the accident.

2. Tell the police officer how the accident happened.

Useful language

Can I see your driver's license, please?

Have you ever had an accident before?

Where | were you going?
How fast |

What did you do | then?
| after that?

Did you see _____ ?

Imagine that you were the driver of the Volkswagen. Write a letter to a friend. Tell your friend about the accident. Begin your letter like this:

Dear _____ ,
    Received your letter last week and was glad to hear from you. How is your new job? How do you like living in the big city?
    A terrible thing happened to me the other day.

Unit Twenty-Five
AWAY FROM HOME

---

1. Read Text 1 of the travel brochure on page 174. Which of these places will you *not* visit? (Cross out three.)

1. United Nations, New York
2. Corning Glass Center, Corning, NY
3. Chocolate World, Hershey, PA
4. Amish farm, Lancaster County, PA
5. White House, Washington, DC
6. Lincoln Memorial, Washington, DC
7. Washington Monument, Washington, DC
8. Independence Hall, Philadelphia, PA
9. Liberty Bell, Philadelphia, PA
10. Betsy Ross House, Philadelphia, PA

COSMOS   East

Niagara Falls and Washington D.C.

Niagara Falls – Penn-Dutch Country – Washington D.C. – Philadelphia

Tour No. **8009**   6 Days from **$269** plus tax
New York to New York

Tour No. **8019**   6 Days from **$259** plus tax
*New York to Washington D.C.

Fully Escorted

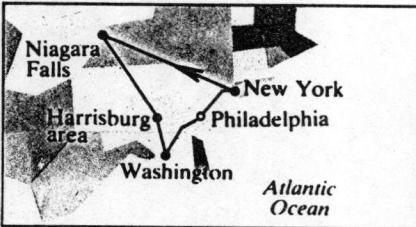

Niagara Falls
Harrisburg area
New York
Philadelphia
Washington
Atlantic Ocean

▲ Amish in Pennsylvania

Day 1   New York – Corning Glass Factory – Finger Lakes – Niagara Falls. The Tour departs at 8 a.m. from the Milford Plaza Hotel, 270 W. 45th Street (at 8th Ave.), heading north and west to Corning to visit the famous Glass Center where Corningware and Steuben glass are made. This afternoon drive through the attractive Finger Lakes country to Niagara Falls. Evening at leisure with an optional excursion to see the Falls floodlit by four million candle power of colored lights.

Day 2   Niagara Falls. Included sightseeing. Your included morning sightseeing tour will show you this spectacular and massive waterfall from various vantage points. For an amazing close-up view from below the thundering waters take an optional boat ride aboard the 'Maid of the Mist.' The rest of the day at leisure.

Day 3   Niagara – Harrisburg area. Head south today following the Susquehanna River, through the Appalachian Mountains and the old Pennsylvania Farm country, to Harrisburg, the state capital. Then to nearby Carlisle for overnight accommodation.

Day 4   Harrisburg area – Hershey – Penn-Dutch Country – Washington D.C. This morning visit 'Chocolatetown U.S.A.' to hear the amazing story of Milton Hershey's success and to visit his Chocolate World. Then to Lancaster County home of the Amish and Mennonite communities. Stop at an Amish farm, where faith and tradition forbid the use of electricity or telephones in the home and promote a distinctive style of dress, family life and the use of horse-drawn buggies in place of motor vehicles. Later this afternoon drive to Washington D.C. and your hotel for the next two nights.

Day 5   Morning Washington city sightseeing. Afternoon at leisure. First this morning an included escorted tour of the great nation's capital; the White House, Capitol Hill and the Lincoln Memorial. Then across the Potomac River to see the American heroes' graves, including John F. Kennedy and his brother Robert in the beautiful Arlington Cemetery. Afternoon free for optional excursions.

Day 6   Washington – Philadelphia – New York. *You may terminate this tour in Washington D.C. this morning. See Departure/Price Guide for applicable price reduction (Tour No. 8019). Today we visit Philadelphia the traditional birthplace of the U.S., historic Independence Hall and Liberty Bell. From here we travel along the fast New Jersey Turnpike to Kennedy Airport. The coach will continue from the airport to the Milford Plaza Hotel in midtown Manhattan arriving in the early evening.

---

2. Read Text 1 again. Answer the questions.

1. Where will you see how glass is made?

2. Where will you see how chocolate is made?

3. Where will you see a group of people who live without electricity, telephone, and cars?

4. Where will you see the graves of John Kennedy and Robert Kennedy?

5. Where will you spend the night on Day 1?

6. Where will you spend the night on Day 2?

7. Where will you spend the night on Day 3?

8. Where will you spend the night on Day 4?

9. Where will you spend the night on Day 5?

Text 2   *Text 3*

THE TOUR PRICE INCLUDES
- 5 nights accommodation in comfortable, well-known hotels and motels in twin-bedded rooms all with private facilities, air-conditioning and TV. All hotel tax, tips and service charges.
- Services of a uniformed Cosmos escort.
- Transportation on tour by modern, comfortable, air-conditioned Greyhound coach, chartered by Cosmos.
- Porterage for one piece of baggage per person throughout the tour.
- Included sightseeing excursions: Niagara Falls, Penn-Dutch Country, Washington D.C., Philadelphia.

twin beds: two single beds
escort: travel guide
baggage: suitcases

DEPARTURE DATES
Sundays out of New York from Apr 7 to Oct 20; return Friday

PRICES AND TAXES
April 7, 14, 21, 28	$269
May 5, 12, 19, 26	$269
June 2, 9, 16, 23, 30	$279
July 7, 14, 21, 28	$289
Aug 4, 11, 18, 25	$289
Sept 1, 8, 15, 22, 29	$279
Oct 6, 13, 20	$279

Add Tax—$6.47
If terminating in Washington D.C. on Day 6—deduct $10.

SINGLES-SHARES-TRIPLES
Single room supplement:
5 nights $90.
Guaranteed shares also available—see page 7.
Triple room reduction, per person: 5 nights $20.

supplement: extra
reduction: less money

3. Read Texts 2 and 3. Answer the questions. Check (✓) all correct answers.

1. What does the tour price include? (Text 2)

    a. Hotel room with two beds, bathroom, air-conditioning, and television
    b. Breakfast, lunch, and dinner
    c. Somebody from Cosmos who will travel with the group, help with problems, and talk about the different places

d. Travel by bus

e. A bus that will take you from your home to the Milford Plaza Hotel

f. Somebody who will carry one of your suitcases

2. What day of the week do the tours begin? (Text 3)

3. What day of the week do the tours end? (Text 3)

4. How much will the trip cost if you go on August 4th? (Text 3)

5. How much will the trip cost if you go on October 20th but do not go to Philadelphia? (Text 3)

6. How much will you pay if you stay in a hotel room alone from April 7th to April 12th? (Text 3)

7. How much will you pay altogether for the tour if you stay in a hotel room with two other people from April 7th to April 12th? (Text 3)

Mr. and Mrs. Mitchell want to go on the Cosmos tour from New York to Washington. Mr. Mitchell calls the travel agency to make reservations for his wife and himself. Act out the conversation he has with the travel agent, Rita Baretta.

Student A

Mr. Mitchell

Say that you and your wife are interested in the tour from New York to Washington. Say when you want to go. Ask if meals are included and how many other people usually go on the tour. Ask if you have to send a deposit. Make sure you have the correct address of the Travel Agency.

STUDENT B: Turn to page 206.

Another couple, Lynn and Harold Christenson, also want to go on the trip.
They get in touch with the travel agency by mail.

1. Read the letter. (You will notice some mistakes.)

City Travel
53 Sumner St.
Hartford, CT 06105

Harold Christenson
26 Woodland St.
Hartford, CT 06105

Dear sir or madam.

Reason for writing

My wife and I are interested in going on the six-day Cosmos bus tour from New York to Washington and Philadelphia. We would like to go on April 21st and return the following Friday.

Request

The brochure does not mention anything about meals. Are they included in the price? If not, how much extra will meals cost? There is also no information about reservations. We would like to know if it is necessary to send a deposit. Finally, could you send us more information about the places we will visit?

Closing

Thank you. We look forward to your reply.

Harold Christensen

2. There are five mistakes in the format of the letter. Can you find them?

3. Imagine that you are going to take a trip. Write a letter to a travel agency or government tourist office and request information.

Photos provided courtesy of Washington Convention and Visitors Association.

Listen to a tour guide explain travel plans to a group of tourists. Fill in the missing parts of the itinerary.

Itinerary — Day 5

_____ Pick up at your hotel.

10:00   Visit, _____ , home of every American president since

_____ . See the famous Green Room, Blue Room, and

Red Room and the beautiful Rose Garden.

_____ Lunch

_____ Short visit to the Smithsonian Institution, made up of

_____ museums. Visit the National Air and Space

Museum to see the Spirit of St. Louis, Gemini IV, and a piece of

_____ rock brought back from one of the first voyages to

the moon.

3:00   Stop at the Washington Monument, built in honor of _____

_____ . At 555 feet 5 inches high, it is the _____

building in Washington. There are _____ stairs, but to

go to the top take the elevator.

3:45   On to the Lincoln Memorial, built in honor of Abraham Lincoln

in _____ . The _____-foot statue is one of the

most famous in the country.

4:30   Cross the Potomac River and visit Arlington Cemetery, where

_____ soldiers and other famous Americans, including

JFK and RFK, are buried. Also visit the Tomb of the Unknown

Soldier.

_____ Return to hotel.

Imagine that you and the other people in your group work for a travel
agency. Plan a two-day visit for tourists to your city. Decide what they
should visit and why. Also decide how long they should spend at each
place.

Useful language

How about taking them to _____ in the afternoon?

I think they should _____ .

In the morning | they should _____ .

| we can take them to _____ .

What do you think they should do in the afternoon?

What | will | they do | then?
| should | | next?
| | | after that?

But what will they | do there?
| like about that place?

Don't you think they'll like _____ more?

1. Read the itinerary on page 178 again.

2. Write up your group's two-day itinerary. Include what the visitors will see and how long they will spend at each place. Also include one or two sentences about why the place is famous and/or interesting.

Unit Twenty-Six
AT SCHOOL

1. The first sentence in this unit's reading is "Drowning is a major cause of accidental death in the United States."

Eight of the words below are from the reading. Four are not. Decide which four words are *not* in the reading. Does your partner agree with your choices?

a. ball   g. help
b. breathe   h. house
c. calm   i. medical
d. car   j. panicked
e. clothes   k. pool
f. cough   l. water

2. Choose the correct answer.

1. *Use extreme caution* (line 5) means

   a. be very careful
   b. look for help quickly

2. *avoid direct contact* (line 5) means

   a. do not touch
   b. do not look at

3. *as well* (line 6) means

   a. good
   b. also

Drowning

Drowning is a major cause of accidental death in the United States. Victims who die of drowning can die within about 4 to 6 minutes of the accident because they have stopped breathing.

1. Get the victim out of the water at once.

5   Use extreme caution to avoid direct contact with the victim, since a panicked victim may drown the rescuer as well.

• If the victim is conscious, push a floating object to him/her or let the victim grasp a long branch, pole or object.

10   • If the victim is unconscious, take a flotation device with you if possible and approach the victim with caution. Once ashore or on the deck of a pool, the victim should be placed on his/her back.

2. If the victim is not breathing, start mouth to mouth rescue breathing immediately. (See Rescue Breathing section.)

15   Keep giving rescue breathing until the victim can breathe unassisted. That can take an hour or two. Pace yourself. Keep calm. Remember: Even when the victim is breathing unassisted, he or she may be in need of medical attention. Have someone

20   else go for help. Do not leave the victim alone under any circumstances . . . not even to call for help!

3. If the victim is breathing without assistance, even though coughing and sputtering, he or she will get rid of the remaining water. You need only stand by to see that recovery continues, but

25   have someone else send for professional help immediately.

---

victim: a person who is hurt
panicked: frightened, scared
rescuer: a person who saves another person
float: to stay on the surface of the water

4. *grasp* (line 8) means

    a. find
    b. hold

5. *unconscious* (line 10) means

    a. awake
    b. not awake

6. *approach* (line 11) means

    a. call
    b. go near

7. *Once ashore* (line 12) means

    a. when the victim is in the water
    b. when the victim is out of the water

8. *Keep* (lines 16 and 17) means

    a. stop
    b. continue

9. *under any circumstances* (lines 20 and 21) means

    a. never
    b. for one minute

10. *stand by* (line 24) means

    a. leave
    b. stay near

3. Find the words that are similar in meaning to the words on the left.

1. *because* (line 3)   _____   (line 5)

2. *immediately* (line 15)   _____ _____   (line 4)

3. *medical attention* (line 19)   _____ _____   (line 25)

4. *help* (line 21)   _____   (line 22)

4. Choose the correct answers to complete this conversation between a swimming instructor and a student. Underline the part of the text that tells you the answer.

Student: Why does the person have to get air?

Instructor: Because drowning victims die when they have

_____ .

    a. gone under water
    b. stopped breathing

Student: What should I do if I see someone drowning?

Instructor: You should _____ , but be

    a. get the person out of the water
    b. call for help

careful because a drowning person is very _____

    a. afraid
    b. strong

and can drown you too.

Student: And then what should I do?

Instructor: Well, then you have to see if the victim is _____

    a. breathing
    b. conscious

or not.

Student: And if the victim is not breathing?

Instructor: You have to start giving mouth-to-mouth rescue breathing at once. You have to do this until the

_____ .

a. doctor comes
b. victim breathes without help

Student: And what about people who are breathing when I take them out of the water? If I think they need a doctor, should I go and get one?

Instructor: _____ .

a. Yes, if you need a doctor, you should go and get one.
b. No, if you need a doctor, someone else should go and get one.

Student: And is the same true for a person who is not breathing?

Instructor: Absolutely.

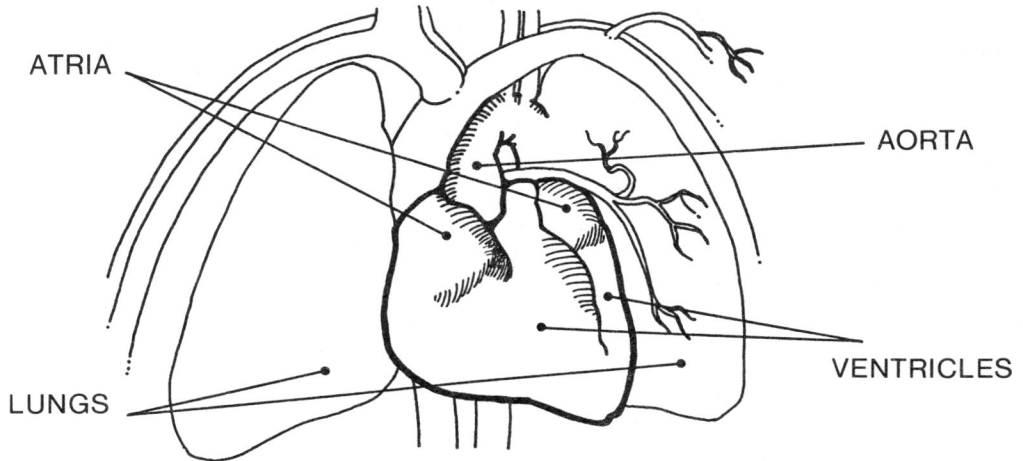

1. Listen to a short lecture on the human heart. Put a number next to the topics in the order that the lecturer talks about them.

_____ . How the heart works

_____ . Parts of the heart

_____ . Function of the heart

_____ . Description of the heart

_____ . Position of the heart

2. Listen to the first part of the lecture. Read along with the notes.

Position of heart:
Muscle. Pumps blood all parts of body. If stops, body does not get oxygen blood carries.

Description of heart:
About size of fist. Man's 11 ounces, woman's 9 ounces. Adult heart—5 inches long, 3-1/2 inches wide, 2-1/2 inches thick. Normal heart beats

70 times minute and more than 100,000 times a day. 10 pints blood go through every 60 seconds.

3. Listen to the next part of the lecture. Complete the missing parts of the notes.

Position of heart:

Lies near _____ of chest between lungs. Wider at_____ than at bottom. Wider part points toward _____ shoulder. Narrower end points toward _____ .

Parts of heart:

Divided into _____ and right sides and _____ and bottom. At_____ two atria. At bottom are_____ . Atria collect _____ that comes to heart through veins. Ventricles larger than atria. Pump_____ into arteries so blood can go to all parts of body.

How heart works:

Blood enters _____ side of heart with CO_2 in it. First goes to _____ _____ , then right ventricle, then_____ . There CO_2 removed from blood and blood gets fresh _____ .

4. Listen to the rest of the lecture. Take notes. In this section the speaker talks about what happens to the blood after it gets fresh oxygen from the lungs.

1. Read this description of the heart. It is from the first part of the lecture notes.

The heart is a muscle that pumps blood to all parts of the body. If it stops, the body does not get the oxygen that the blood carries.

The heart is about the size of a fist. A man's heart weighs about 11 ounces and a woman's around 9 ounces. The adult heart is approximately 5 inches long, 3-1/2 inches wide, and 2-1/2 inches thick. A normal heart beats 70 times a minute and more than 100,000 times a day. 10 pints of blood go through it every 60 seconds.

2. Use your notes on the position of the heart, the parts of the heart, and how it works to write a composition.

Imagine that you have taken these notes during a lecture. Your partner was absent that day and calls you. Give him or her the notes.

Student A (Lungs)

Function — pumps air into & out of body (supply body with O_2 and remove CO_2)

Description — *number*, 2; *color*, gray; *location*, in chest on each side of heart; *size*, right lung, 13–19 oz. (375–550 g.), left lung, 11.5–16 oz. (325–450 g.)

How they work — a. air enters lungs from nose & windpipe (trachea) — chest gets bigger; b. air leaves lungs — chest gets smaller

This process (air entering & leaving lungs) happens about 16 times a minute — faster than 16 when body needs more O_2, e.g., when someone is running

---

STUDENT B: Turn to page 207.

Use the notes your partner gave you to write a short description.

Are the students in your class from different countries? If so, do Sections A and B. If everyone in your class is from the same country, do not do Section A.

Section A

Educational systems are different all over the world. Fill in the first line of the chart with information about the educational system in your country. Then ask the others in your group about education in their country. Fill in the chart with this information:

a. How many years children must go to school (from what age)

b. How many years people go to elementary school, junior high school and high school

c. What subjects they have to study in junior high and high school

d. How students get into university (Are there entrance exams? What subjects are on the exam?)

Useful language (school subjects)

Math (Algebra, Geometry, Calculus)   Music
Science (Biology, Chemistry, Physics)   Art
History   Religion
Foreign Languages   Physical Education: phys. ed.

COUNTRY	Number of years at school	Years at elementary school (Ages)	Years at junior high school (Ages)	Years at high school (Ages)	Subjects at junior high school	Subjects at high school	University Entrance

Section B

Talk about your memories of school.

    a. What was your favorite subject? Why?

    b. What was your worst subject? Why?

    c. Who was your favorite teacher? Why?

    d. Who was your worst teacher? Why?

    e. What are your best memories?

    f. What are your worst memories?

Useful language

I liked her because her classes were interesting.
she | was kind.
was easy.
gave good grades.
always helped me.

I didn't like him because he | was very strict.
punished me a lot.
gave lots of homework.
couldn't teach.

I was | good at _____ .

terrible at _____ .

Unit Twenty-Seven
IN THE NEWS

1. You are going to read the first part of an article that appeared in the *International Herald Tribune*. (See page 192.) Look at the headline from the article. Answer the questions.

   1. What is the article about?

   2. Do you know when the event happened?

   3. Do you know how the event happened?

   4. What do you think *riot* means?

2. Read the article quickly. Fill in the chart.

Number dead	
Number injured	
Number of injured in critical condition	
When the fighting began	

40 Killed, 250 Injured As Soccer Fans Riot at Cup Match in Brussels

Compiled by Our Staff From Dispatches

BRUSSELS — At least 40 persons were killed and more than 250 were injured Wednesday night when rioting broke out at Heysel Stadium 15 before the start of the European Soccer Cup
5 final between Liverpool and Juventus of Turin, police and Red Cross officials said.

Police said that 15 to 20 of the injured were in critical condition.

Witnesses said that many of the dead were
10 trampled when British fans surged into a section of the stands occupied by Italian supporters, forcing the Italians against a concrete dividing wall that collapsed under the onrush of pan-icked spectators.

Police and hospital officials were unable to say whether most of the dead were British or Italian. Police said that the majority of fans involved in the violence were from Liverpool.

The disturbances began an hour before the
20 start of play. Organizers ordered that the match go ahead, apparently because they feared fur-ther rioting if it were canceled.

Juventus won, 1-0.

---

trample: to step on other people with your feet
surge: to move quickly together at the same time
onrush: many people moving forward together at the same time

---

3. Match the words on the left with their meaning on the right.

1. witnesses (line 9)	a. very afraid
2. collapse (line 13)	b. clean
3. panicked (lines 13 and 14)	c. people who see something happen
4. majority (line 17)	d. fall
5. violence (line 18)	e. begin
6. go ahead (line 21)	f. the largest number
	g. fighting, killing

4. Find the words that are similar in meaning to the words on the left.

1. *began* (line 19) _____ _____ (lines 1 to 3)

2. *fans* (line 10) _____ (lines 11 to 13)

3. *rioting* (line 3) _____ (lines 19 to 21)

5. Put these sentences in the correct order.

_____ a. The fans arrived at the stadium.

_____ b. The Italians were afraid and ran.

_____ c. Juventus of Turin won the game.

_____ d. A dividing wall made of concrete fell on a group of Italian fans.

_____ e. The soccer match began.

_____ f. Liverpool fans ran into a section of the stands where the Italians were sitting.

6. Put a check (✓) if the text has this information.

1. How the people were killed or injured.

2. How many people watched the match.

3. Who started the fighting.

4. Why the game was played after the violence and deaths.

5. Which team won the game.

6. What will probably happen to British soccer teams because of the violence.

7. How many police were at Heysel Stadium.

Newspapers and magazines sometimes report different facts about the same event.

1. Look at the facts on page 194 about the Heysel Stadium rioting which come from three newspapers and two magazines.

I.H.T. = International Herald Tribune
T = The Times (of London)
N.Y.T. = The New York Times

	I.H.T.	T	N.Y.T.	Time	Newsweek
Number killed	At least 40	At least 38	More than 40	38	At least 38
Number injured	More than 250	More than 70	More than 100	425	More than 40
Number of people at stadium	✕	58,000	✕	58,000	60,000
Number of police at stadium	2,000	✕	✕	1,000	960
When fighting began	7:15	7:30	✕	7:30	7:20

2. Look at these sentences which compare one of the differences between the *International Herald Tribune* and *The Times* reports.

a. The *International Herald Tribune* said that at least 40 people were killed, *but The Times* said that at least 38 people were killed.

b. The *Tribune* said that at least 40 people were killed. *However, The Times* said that at least 38 people were killed.

c. The *Tribune* said that at least 40 people were killed. *On the other hand, The Times* said that at least 38 people were killed.

d. *Although* the *Herald Tribune* said that at least 40 people were killed, *The Times* said that at least 38 people were killed.

e. *While* the *Herald Tribune* said that at least 40 people were killed, *The Times* said that at least 38 people were killed.

3. Write sentences about the other differences between the reports. Use these words to help you:

but	although
however	while
on the other hand	

Match the famous names with their well-known quotations. Discuss the answers with your partner. Give reasons for your choices. See the bottom of page 197 for the answers.

1. Woody Allen, American comedy actor and film director

2. Marie Antoinette, French queen just before the French revolution

3. Aristotle, ancient Greek philosopher

4. Neil Armstrong, American astronaut

5. Julius Caesar, Roman emperor

6. Winston Churchill, British prime minister

7. Amelita Galli-Curci, Italian opera singer

8. John Lennon, British rock star and member of the Beatles

9. Joe Namath, American football star

10. Elvis Presley, American rock 'n' roll star

11. Franklin D. Roosevelt, American president

   a. "Happiness depends upon ourselves."
   b. "I came, I saw, I conquered.[1]"
   c. "I don't know anything about music. In my line[2] you don't have to."
   d. "It's not that I'm afraid to die. I just don't want to be there when it happens."
   e. "Let them eat cake!"
   f. "Nobody really sings in an opera. They just make loud noises."
   g. "One small step for man, one giant leap[3] for mankind."
   h. ". . . the only thing we have to fear is fear itself."
   i. "Those of you in the cheaper seats clap[4] your hands. Those of you in the more expensive ones rattle[5] your jewelry."
   j. "We shall defend our island, whatever the cost may be, we shall fight on the beaches, we shall fight on the landing grounds, we shall fight in the fields and in the streets, we shall fight in the hills; we shall never surrender.[6]"
   k. "When you win, nothing hurts.[7]"

[1]conquer: to win, to gain by force
[2]line: business, profession
[3]leap: a large step
[4]clap: to bring the hands together to make a loud noise
[5]rattle: to shake an object to make a loud noise
[6]surrender: to lose a fight, to give up
[7]hurt: to cause or feel pain

Imagine you are a reporter. You have the headline and first sentence of your article. You need to get the rest of the information.

Listen to the news broadcast about the report of strange creatures. The broadcast will give you information you will need for your news article. Listen for the information below and write it down in note form:

  a. What the occupations of the people who made the report were

  b. How old the people who made the report were

  c. What time they saw the creatures

  d. How tall the creatures were

  e. How the creatures "talked" to each other

  f. What the creatures did when they saw the people

  g. What the people were having for lunch

Listen to the news broadcast again for more information. This time, Student A and Student B will listen for different information. Write down the information in note form:

Student A

  a. Who made the report

  b. Where they saw the creatures

  c. Where the people who made the report were from

  d. How many creatures they saw

Student B

  e. When they saw the creatures

  f. What the creatures looked like

  g. What the people who made the report were doing when they saw the creatures

  h. What they did when they saw the creatures

With your partner, find out the rest of the information to complete your news story. Student A asks Student B questions e to h above. Student B asks Student A questions a to d above. Write down the new information in note form.

Useful language

Do you know where _____ ?

Could you tell me what _____ ?

I was wondering if you could tell me when _____ .
   I'm afraid not.
   I'm afraid I can't.
   I'm sorry. I don't know.

Using all the information you got from the news broadcast and your partners, write the news article. When you are finished, exchange your article with another student and compare the two articles.

Here are the answers to the famous quotations on page 195:

1. d 2. e 3. a 4. g 5. b 6. j 7. f 8. i 9. k 10. c 11. h

Appendix A
STUDENT B
EXERCISES
(for pair work)

Student B — Caller

Name Paula Spenser	Area Code 312	Name John Turner	Area Code 312
Street 1639 W. 16th St.	Phone	Street 3105 N. Kenmore	Phone
City State Zip Code Chicago IL 60608		City State Zip Code Chicago IL 60657	

Student B — Operator

Brown, William	4313 Jefferson Ave	Seattle	286 8320
Browne, William G	722 Cherry	Seattle	242 7935
Chun, R	3618 Whitman Ave N	Seattle	343 4310
Chun, Rose	5547 33 Ave NE	Seattle	689 0326

Student B

1. You are the secretary. Mr. Watson is not in.

2. You are the caller. Your name is Barbara/Bob Tucker. Your telephone number is (903) 652-3091. Call Louise Heller.

3. You are the secretary. Ms. Pappas is in.

4. You are the caller. Your name is Debbie/Don Peters. Your telephone number is 233-1162, extension 72. Call Mr. Paulson.

5. You are the secretary. Mrs. Platt is not in.

6. You are the caller. Your name is Sandy/Steve Lane. Your telephone number is (506) 337-6252. Call George Rivers.

Student B

OLDIES-BUT-GOODIES WEEK

ABC **THE DEERHUNTER with ROBERT DE NIRO and MERYL STREEP.** A film about the war in Vietnam. 3:00 6:00 9:00	Center
Bala **JAWS with RICHARD DREYFUSS and ROY SCHEIDER.** A film about a killer shark. 4:20 6:30 8:40 10:50	Embassy

Student B

Ask your partner for the location of these places:

ABC Movie Theater   Atlantic Hardware
City Laundromat   Jack's Grocery Store
Sweet's Bakery   The University Book Store

| Price Supermarket | | | Abe's Parking Lot | Post Office |

FIRST STREET

Sam's Fruit Store	Tom's Restaurant	Market Street Drugstore		Best Gas Station		Hollywood Cinema
		Tasty Restaurant		Anna's Boutique		
				Green's Record Shop		
		Allen's Shoe Store		World Florist		
		Bell's Dry Cleaners		Lacy's Department Store		
Photo House						

MARKET STREET

| | First City Bank | | |

201

Student B

1. Your partner wants to go to Chicago. This is the travel information:

BUS	Times of Departure	7:20 AM	9:20 AM	1:30 PM	6:30 PM
	Times of Arrival	2:30 PM	4:30 PM	8:30 PM	1:45 AM
	Fare (One-way) $56	(Round-trip) $102			

TRAIN	Times of Departure	6 AM	
	Times of Arrival	10:15 PM	
	Fare (One-way) $85	(Round-trip) $150	

PLANE	Times of Departure	9:30 AM	5:05 PM
	Times of Arrival	10:30 PM	6:05 PM
	Fare (One-way) $180	(Round-trip) $360	

2. You want to go to San Diego. Ask for information.

Student B

	Egypt	Colombia	Thailand	Senegal	
Population	45,111,000		50,284,000		
Area	386,198 sq. mi. (999,730 sq. km.)			75,750 sq. mi. (196,840 sq. km.)	
Capital		Bogota		Dakar	
Highest Point	Jabal Katrinah 8668 ft. (2,642 m.)	Cristobal Colon 19,019 ft. (5,797 m.)			
Longest River		Magdalena	Chao Phrayo		
Currency		peso		CFA	
Language	Arabic			Wolof, Fulani, Mandingo, French	
Major Agricultural Product			rice	peanuts	

Student B

Weather

Abroad

Following are the temperatures and weather conditions in foreign cities yesterday at the local time indicated:

City	Time	Temp	Conditions
Aberdeen	1 P.M.	56	Pt.cldy.
Amsterdam	1 P.M.	64	Cloudy
Ankara	3 P.M.	65	Clear
Athens	2 P.M.		
Auckland	Mdnt.	67	Rain
Beirut	2 P.M.	68	Clear
Berlin	1 P.M.	58	Pt.cldy.
Bonn	1 P.M.	64	Clear
Brussels	1 P.M.	63	Pt.cldy.
Buenos Aires	9 A.M.	62	Clear
Cairo	2 P.M.	81	Clear
Casablanca	Noon		
Copenhagen	1 P.M.	56	Cloudy
Dakar	Noon	71	Pt.cldy.
Dublin	1 P.M.	54	Cloudy
Geneva	1 P.M.	54	Clear
Helsinki	2 P.M.	40	Rain
Hong Kong	8 P.M.		
Jerusalem	2 P.M.		
Lima	7 A.M.		
Lisbon	1 P.M.	63	Cloudy
London	1 P.M.	65	Clear
Madrid	1 P.M.		
Managua	6 A.M.		N.A.
Manila	8 P.M.	84	Pt.cldy.
Montreal	1 P.M.	45	Cloudy
Moscow	3 P.M.		
New Delhi	6 P.M.		
Nice	1 P.M.	62	Cloudy
Oslo	1 P.M.	46	Cloudy
Paris	1 P.M.	66	Clear
Peking	8 P.M.	69	Pt.cldy.
Pretoria	2 P.M.	78	Clear
Rio de Janeiro	9 A.M.		
Riyadh	3 P.M.	96	Clear
Rome	1 P.M.	70	Clear
Seoul	9 P.M.		
Stockholm	1 P.M.	51	Clear
Sydney	10 P.M.	58	Clear
Taipei	8 P.M.	72	Cloudy
Tokyo	9 P.M.		
Toronto	1 P.M.	43	Shwrs.
Vienna	1 P.M.	60	Pt.cldy.
Warsaw	1 P.M.	55	Clear
Winnipeg	1 P.M.	75	Pt.cldy.

Pt. cldy. = partly cloudy
Tstrms. = thunderstorms

Student B

Customer

Ask for the menu. Talk about what to order. Ask the waiter or waitress about any unknown dishes. Give your order.

Useful language

I'd like _____ , please.

Can I have _____ , please?

What is a pizza burger?

What kind of ice cream do you have?

Is it | spicy?
     | sweet?

Student B

Customers

There are four language schools. The owners each want you to come to their school. In groups decide which school is the best.

1. Each member of the group should go to a different owner.

2. Get information about the school.

3. Report to your group what you found out.

4. Decide as a group which school to go to.

When you talk to the owner, find out:

    a. the name of the school
    b. the number of weeks/months per course   (How long?)
    c. the number of class hours a week   (How often?)
    d. tuition (How much?)
    e. the number of students in a class (How many?)
    f. types of courses, e.g., TOEFL preparation
       (Does your school have courses in _____ ?)
    g. facilities at the schol, e.g., language lab
    h. anything else you want to know

Student B

1. Ask your partner questions. Write down the answers. Guess the name of the famous person.

   Nationality: Occupation:
   Date of Birth: Place of Birth:
   Date of Death: Place of Death:
   Reason for being famous:

   Name: _____

2. Answer your partner's questions. Do not say the name of the famous person. (Charlie Chaplin)

   Nationality: British   Occupation: Actor
   Date of Birth: April 16, 1889   Place of Birth: London, England
   Date of Death: Dec. 25, 1977   Place of Death: Switzerland
   Reason for being famous:
       Funny films, funny walk and
       mustache

Student B

Rita Baretta

Ask the customer for his and his wife's name and telephone number and when they want to go. Tell him how much the trip will cost. A deposit is necessary. Tell him how much. Begin the conversation like this:
   "Hello, City Travel. Rita Baretta speaking. May I help you?"

Student B (Blood)

Function — 1. carries O_2 & other nutrients* to parts of body; 2. fights germs†
that enter body

Description — *color*, dark red when not much O_2, e.g., when blood goes to
lungs, bright red when rich in O_2; *amount*, a. about 17 pints (5–6 liters) go
around body constantly; b. contains about 20 billion tiny cells; c. in average
adult, blood 7–8% of body weight

Parts of blood — a. red cells—carry O_2 & other nutrients; b. white cells—fight
germs; c. platelets—make blood become solid, e.g., when a person has a cut;
d. plasma—liquid which carries red cells, white cells, and platelets around
body

How it works — in about 1/2 a minute; a. goes from heart to lungs and back to
heart; b. out of heart through arteries to other parts of body, e.g., the legs;
c. back to heart through veins

*Nutrients: a chemical or food the body needs for life and growth
†Germs: very small living things on food or dirt or in the body which cause disease or sickness

Appendix B
TAPESCRIPTS

Secretary:	Good morning. I want your attention for just a minute. I need all of your names. The director wants to talk to you one at a time. Please come up to the desk and tell me your names and where you're from. Hello. And your name is?
Alvarez:	Antonio Alvarez.
Secretary:	Spell that, please.
Alvarez:	The first name or the last?
Secretary:	Both, please.
Alvarez:	The first name is A N T O N I O.
Secretary:	And the last?
Alvarez:	A L V A R E Z.
Secretary:	A L V A R E Z. And you're from Brazil?
Alvarez:	No, I'm from Mexico.
Secretary:	Oh, Mexico. I'm sorry. Okay. Please sit down. The director sees you first.
Alvarez:	Okay, thanks.
Secretary:	Next, please.
Calafati:	Hello. My name is Maria Calafati. C A L A F A T I. And I'm from Greece.
Secretary:	I'm sorry. Spell that again, please.
Calafati:	C A L A F A T I.
Secretary:	And you're from Greece?
Calafati:	That's right.
Secretary:	All right, thank you. And your name is?
Morimoto:	Keiko Morimoto.
Secretary:	How do you spell the first name?
Morimoto:	K E I K O.
Secretary:	Is that K E I or K I E?
Morimoto:	That's K E I K O, and the last name is M O R I M O T O.
Secretary:	M O R I M O T O. And you're from Japan?
Morimoto:	Yes, Tokyo.
Secretary:	Thank you, Ms. Morimoto. And what's your name, sir?
Nur:	Hakim Nur.

Secretary:	Hakim is the first name?
Nur:	Yes, that's H A K I M. And the last name's N U R.
Secretary:	N U R. And you say Nur?
Nur:	Uh-huh.
Secretary:	And where are you from, Mr. Nur?
Nur:	Cairo, Egypt.
Secretary:	Egypt. Okay, fine. Have a seat for a few minutes.
Nur:	Thank you.
Secretary:	Next please.

Unit Two

Operator:	Hello. What city, please?
Caller:	Hello, operator. Boston, please. The number for Mary White. She lives on Beacon Street.
Operator:	Just a minute, please. The number is 272-5052.
Caller:	272-5052?
Operator:	Yes, that's right.
Caller:	Thank you.
Operator:	You're welcome.

Operator:	Good evening. What city, please?
Caller:	Philadelphia. The name is Mancini.
Operator:	How do you spell that, please?
Caller:	M A N C I N I.
Operator:	Thank you. I have a Jerry Mancini at 985 Lancaster Avenue. The number is 468-9301.
Caller:	Did you say 9310?
Operator:	No, 9301. That's 468-9301.
Caller:	Thanks very much.
Operator:	Have a nice evening.

Operator:	Good morning. What city, please?
Caller:	I'd like the number for a Doctor Gold.
Operator:	Excuse me. What city do you want?
Caller:	Oh, I'm sorry. Atlanta.
Operator:	And the name is?
Caller:	Gold. G O L D.
Operator:	Thank you. There is a Doctor Susan Gold on Greenwillow Drive and a Doctor P. Gold on Edgewood Avenue.
Caller:	I want Dr. Susan Gold.
Operator:	The number is 531-0320.
Caller:	531-0320. Thank you.

Operator:	You're welcome. Have a nice day.
Caller:	You too.

Operator:	Hello. What city, please?
Caller:	Sheridan. The number for T. J. Hudson.
Operator:	Is that T as in Tom or D as in dog?
Caller:	T as in Tom.
Operator:	Thank you. I have listings for a T. Hudson, a Thomas Hudson, and a Timothy Hudson.
Caller:	I'm sorry, but I don't know the first name.
Operator:	Do you know the address?
Caller:	Let me see. Yes, it's 1226 Pioneer Road.
Operator:	I have a Timothy Hudson at that address.
Caller:	That's it.
Operator:	The number is 436-7851.
Caller:	I'm sorry. Could you repeat that, please?
Operator:	That's 436-7851.
Caller:	436-7851. Thank you very much.
Operator:	You're welcome.

Unit Three

Susan:	Jack, are there more bills to pay?
Jack:	Just two, the electric and the rent.
Susan:	All right. I should make the electric bill out to City Electric, right?
Jack:	Yeah.
Susan:	And what's the date today? November 8th?
Jack:	That's right.
Susan:	How much is the bill?
Jack:	Let's see. Total amount due: 35 dollars and 12 cents.
Susan:	$35.12, and for nothing!
Jack:	Just write the check. Don't complain! And the second check is for 500 and 75 dollars.
Susan:	Hold on. I'm not finished with the check to City Electric.
Jack:	Boy, are you slow!
Susan:	Okay, okay, you said the rent is 500 and 55?
Jack:	No, I said 500 and 75. What, you still don't know how much rent we pay!
Susan:	Just tell me who I make the check out to.
Jack:	Mary Simpson.
Susan:	How do you spell Simpson?
Jack:	What a good speller you are! S I M P S O N.
Susan:	Okay. Mary Simpson. 575 dollars. Is that it for the month?

Jack:	Yeah, that's it. But let's go over our budget. We never have enough money these days.
Susan:	Okay. There's 500 and 75 for rent and this month 35 dollars and 12 cents for electricity. What else?
Jack:	Let's see. Uh. 22 for the phone, 10 dollars for water.
Susan:	And how much did we spend for food?
Jack:	Wait, let me add it up. 250.
Susan:	That's a lot. We have to cut down. And how much was the gas for heat?
Jack:	48 dollars and 16 cents. Uh. And let's add up how much we spent for entertainment.
Susan:	8 dollars for the movies and, hmm, 45 when we took your mother out for dinner, and . . . uh . . . another 7 for your ticket to the baseball game. That makes . . . uh . . . 60 dollars.
Jack:	Is that everything?
Susan:	Yeah. Oh, no. We forgot the car. 90 dollars for gas and 83 for insurance. That makes a total of . . . let's see . . . 173 dollars total for the car. That's it.
Jack:	So, what have we got?
Susan:	575 for rent, 35 dollars and 12 cents for electricity, 22 for the phone, 10 for water, uh, 250 for food, 48.16 for heat, entertainment was 60 dollars, and the car cost us 173.
Jack:	Do you want to total it up, or should I?
Susan:	Be my guest.
Jack:	Incredible!
Susan:	Well, what is it? What's the bad news?
Jack:	1173 dollars and 28 cents. We have to cut down!
Susan:	You're not kidding! Maybe if we . . .

Unit Four

Secretary:	Good morning. Workman Company. Can I help you?
Caller:	Uh . . . yeah. Hi. Is Susie there?
Secretary:	You have the wrong number.
Caller:	Oh, sorry.
Secretary:	Good morning. Workman Company. Can I help you?
Mr. Suzuki:	Yes. Good morning. This is Mr. Suzuki from Video TV. Could I speak to Mr. Workman, please?
Secretary:	I'm sorry, but Mr. Workman is out at the moment. Can I take a message?
Mr. Suzuki:	Uh, yes, okay. Tell him John Suzuki called. That's S U Z U K I.

Secretary:	Yes.
Mr. Suzuki:	From Video TV.
Secretary:	Yes, Video TV.
Mr. Suzuki:	Tell him I telephoned. I'd like to see him about the video tapes. Can he call me this afternoon?
Secretary:	Yes, of course. What's your telephone number?
Mr. Suzuki:	It's area code 413, 447-9626.
Secretary:	447-9662?
Mr. Suzuki:	No, 447-9626.
Secretary:	Oh, I'm sorry, 447-9626.
Mr. Suzuki:	Yes, that's right, extension 162.
Secretary:	Extension 162. Okay, Mr. Suzuki. I'll give him the message.
Mr. Suzuki:	Thank you. Good-bye.
Secretary:	Good-bye. Okay, let's see. Where's the memo pad? And it's September 19th, at 10:30 . . .
Secretary:	Good morning, Workman Company. Can I help you?
Caller:	Susie? Is that you?
Secretary:	No! You have the wrong number. Please check it.
Caller:	Oh, sorry.
Secretary:	Hello.
Alice Spencer:	Hello. I'd like to speak to Mr. Gonzalez, please.
Secretary:	Who's calling, please?
Alice:	My name is Alice Spencer.
Secretary:	Hold on, please.
Alice:	Thank you.
Secretary:	Hello.
Ray Massey:	Hello, can I speak to Mr. Hennessey, please?
Secretary:	I'm sorry. He's not here. Can I take a message?
Ray:	Yes, please tell him to call Ray Massey. It's important.
Secretary:	How do you spell your last name?
Ray:	M A S S E Y.
Secretary:	Is that M as in Michael?
Ray:	Yes, that's right.
Secretary:	And what's your telephone number?
Ray:	Area code 215, 627-9932.
Secretary:	All right. I'll give him the message.
Ray:	Thank you.

Unit Five

Hello. This is a recorded message from the Manor Twin Cinemas, located at 729 Murray Avenue in Squirrel Hill. Monday and Tuesday are our bargain nights. All seats are two dollars. Wednesday through Sunday, all seats are five dollars. In Cinema one we're pleased to present *Firstborn*, rated PG-13, a suspenseful drama starring Terri Garr. Show times this evening will be at 7:45 and 9:45. Don't miss *Firstborn*.

In Cinema two we're pleased to present Diane Keaton and Klaus Kinski in *The Little Drummer Girl*, rated R. Show times this evening will be 7:30 and 10 o'clock. Free parking is available at indoor garages on either side of the theater. Thank you for calling the Manor Twin Cinemas and have a nice day.

Rachel: Hello. Cinema World. Rachel speaking. Can I help you?
Caller: Yes. Can you tell me the times *Year of the Dragon* is playing today?
Rachel: The first show is at 2:00, then 4:30, 7:00, 9:30, and a late show at 11:00.
Caller: Nothing before two o'clock?
Rachel: No, afraid not.
Caller: And how much are the tickets?
Rachel: Two dollars for the two o'clock matinee and four dollars and fifty cents for the other performances.
Caller: Two dollars for the two o'clock show and $4.50 for the others. Right. Thank you very much.
Rachel: You're welcome and thank you for calling Cinema World.

Unit Six

Mrs. O'Malley: Good morning, Mrs. Rivera.
Mrs. Rivera: Good morning.
Mrs. O'Malley: Are you and your family settled in now?
Mrs. Rivera: Yes, finally, thank you.
Mrs. O'Malley: And how do you like Pleasantville?
Mrs. Rivera: It seems very nice and quiet. I want to find out where things are in the town.
Mrs. O'Malley: Well, that's not difficult in Pleasantville. You can see everything on one walk down Main Street. Let me tell you what you'll find on the part of Main Street near us. Now, if

you have any problems—and I don't think you will—call or go to the police station on the corner of First and Main. The post office is next to the police station and across the street from A & H Hardware Store. Now, walk up Main, past the park, the library, and the town hall. There's a nice little restaurant right past the park on the corner of Main and Second. It's on the right-hand side of the street.

Mrs. Rivera: Does the restaurant serve breakfast, lunch, and dinner?

Mrs. O'Malley: No, just breakfast and lunch. On Fourth and Main is the, uh, Big Apple Supermarket. It's on the same side as the library and the town hall. It's a pretty big store and it has just about everything.

Mrs. Rivera: Uh, good.

Mrs. O'Malley: The Town Movie Theater is right across the street from the supermarket, on the left, no, on the right-hand corner of Fourth and Main as you come, hmm, as you come from the park. Uh. Let's see. Uh. Is there anything else on Main before Fourth? Oh yes, there's that lovely little hotel. It's between the restaurant and the movie theater. You can't miss it. It's a lovely little hotel with lots of gorgeous flowers in front. Now if you continue down Main. . .

Mrs. Rivera: Excuse me, Mrs. O'Malley. You are very kind and helpful but I have to go. I have something on the stove.

Mrs. O'Malley: Well, I see. Just remember, if you need anything, be sure to let me know.

Mrs. Rivera: I'll be sure to. Thanks.

Unit Seven

Conversation 1

Customer: Excuse me. What time does the next train for Johnstown leave?

Ticket agent: At 8:15.

Customer: And what platform does it leave from?

Ticket agent: Let's see . . . platform 7.

Customer: And how long does the trip take?

Ticket agent: About two hours.

Customer: Thank you.

Customer: Good evening. I have a reservation for this evening's flight to Guadalajara.

Ticket agent: Can I have your ticket, please?

Customer: Here you are.

Ticket agent:	Would you like smoking or nonsmoking?
Customer:	Nonsmoking, please.
Ticket agent:	Okay. Here you are, sir. Your seat number is 37F.
Customer:	Is that in a nonsmoking area?
Ticket agent:	Yes, it is, sir. Your plane will be boarding at gate 13 at 6:45.
Customer:	Gate 13 at 6:45. Fine. Thank you.
Ticket agent:	You're welcome, sir. Have a good trip.
Customer:	Excuse me. When's the next bus to Akron?
Ticket agent:	At 12:00.
Customer:	Can I have two tickets, please?
Ticket agent:	One-way or round-trip?
Customer:	One-way, please.
Ticket agent:	That'll be $25.50.
Customer:	Thank you.
Ticket agent:	You're welcome.

Unit Eight

Good afternoon. My name is Sandra Clifton, and I am the teacher for this course on William Shakespeare. This is English Literature, 201, the Works of William Shakespeare. Now on your desks there is a list of the homework assignments for the course. Has everyone got one? Good. Before we begin talking about the life and times of William Shakespeare, I'd like to go over the homework assignments. Uh, there are one or two mistakes and a couple of changes.

Let's start at the beginning. The first week is okay. But for week two, please read pages 1 to 78 of *Macbeth*, not 1 to 55. Okay? Have you got that? For week two, then, read 1 to 78, and week three, 79 to the end. Now, uh, I'd also like to change the order of what you read. We're going to do *Henry V* before *Romeo and Juliet* and the midterm. So week four is *Henry V*, pages 1 to 59 and week five is *Henry V*, 60 to the end. Week six is the midern. No change there. Week seven we'll do *Romeo and Juliet*, pages 1 to 85, and week eight, 86 to the end. On week nine, we begin the final work of the course, *Hamlet*. Please change pages 1 to 69 to pages 1 to 93. And for week ten, pages 94 to the end. And finally, the dates of the last two weeks are wrong. Thanksgiving is on November twenty-first; so there is no class then. The date for week ten is November 28th and the date of week eleven, that's the week of the final exam, is December 5th. Hmm.

Now let me go through the changes again. Week two, *Macbeth*, 1 to 78. Week three, 79 to the end. Weeks four and five, *Henry V*. Weeks seven and eight, *Romeo and Juliet*, same pages. Week nine, *Hamlet*, pages 1 to 93 and week ten, pages 94 to the end. Change the date for the tenth week to November 28th and the date for the final exam to December 5th. Okay? Any questions? Yes?

Unit Nine

This is *News on the Hour*, Ed Wilson reporting. The President and First Lady will visit Africa on a goodwill tour in May. They plan to visit eight African countries.

Reports from China say the Chinese want closer ties between China and the U.S. and Western Europe. A group of top Chinese scientists starts its ten-nation tour next month.

Here in Miami, the mayor is still meeting with the leaders of the teachers' union to try to find a solution to the strike. City schools are still closed after two weeks.

In news about health, scientists in California report findings of a relationship between the drinking of coffee and the increase of heart disease among women. According to the report in the *American Medical Journal*, the five-year study shows this: women who drink more than two cups of coffee a day have a greater chance of having heart disease than women who do not.

In sports, the Chargers lost again last night. The BBs beat them 1 to nothing with a homerun by Mike Thompson. The Wingers had better results. They beat the Rifles 7 to 3. It was their first win in their last five outings.

The weather outlook for Miami—partly cloudy and cool with temperatures in the low seventies. The overnight low will be in the midfifties. Expected high tomorrow in the low seventies. The current temperature outside our studio, 71 degrees. That's 21 on the Celsius scale. And now back to more easy listening with Jan Singer.

ROUND TWO
Unit Ten

Donna: Hello.
Ron: Hello. I'd like to speak to Donna, please.
Donna: Speaking.
Ron: Oh, hello, Donna. My name is Ron Horton. Frank asked me to call you.
Donna: Why? Is anything wrong?
Ron: No, no. It's just that Frank won't have time to take you to the party. So I will instead.
Donna: You sure that won't be too much trouble for you?

Ron: No, no trouble.
Donna: Shall we meet at the same time and place?
Ron: Yeah. At 6:30 on the corner of 53rd and Arlington. Right?
Donna: Right.
Ron: Okay, see you then.
Donna: No, wait. How will I recognize you?
Ron: Well, I'm tall and thin—the man of your dreams.
Donna: No, seriously.
Ron: I'm about 6 feet tall and thin. I have blond hair, blue eyes, and a
           mustache. And let's see. I'll be wearing a brown jacket and jeans. And
           don't worry. I'll recognize you. Frank has shown me your picture at
           least 30 times.
Donna: Okay, Ron. See you then at 6:30.
Ron: Looking forward to it. Bye-bye.
Donna: Bye.

Unit Eleven

Arthur: I'm going out to get a paper. Do you want anything?
Jenny: Yeah, just a few things. Get a dozen eggs.
Arthur: Wait a second. I want to write this down. Eggs . . . okay.
Jenny: Butter.
Arthur: Yeah.
Jenny: Milk.
Arthur: Uh-huh.
Jenny: And get a small bag of flour. I'm going to bake a cake. And some
           sugar.
Arthur: Flour and sugar. Anything else?
Jenny: Let me check the refrigerator. Oh, yeah, some fruit. Get three or
           four apples and a few oranges. And while you're at it, get some
           bananas too.
Arthur: Apples, oranges, bananas. I thought you only wanted a few things.
Jenny: Oh, and we don't have anything for a salad. Get a head of lettuce, a
           tomato or two, and a green pepper. Oh, yeah, and some onions too.
Arthur: Lettuce, tomatoes, green pepper, onions. What else?
Jenny: That's all. I did say just a few things.
Arthur: Let me make sure I got everything: eggs, butter, milk, flour, sugar,
           apples, oranges, bananas, lettuce, tomatoes, green pepper, onions.
           Is that all?
Jenny: Well, maybe I'll check the freezer.
Arthur: No, that's okay. Check it another time. I don't want to spend all day
           shopping for your "few things."

Unit Twelve

Ben Richards:	Good morning. Tannenbaum and Minsk. Ben Richards speaking.
Jeannie Campbell:	Hello. I'm calling about the two-bedroom apartment advertised in today's *Daily News*. Is it still available?
Ben:	Uh. Yes, it is.
Jeannie:	What's the rent?
Ben:	$500 a month including heat and hot water.
Jeannie:	And what floor is the apartment on?
Ben:	The sixth.
Jeannie:	The sixth. That's good. Are the bedrooms a good size?
Ben:	One bedroom is very large. The other one is much smaller, good for a child, if you have one.
Jeannie:	Oh no. The apartment is just for myself and my husband. Tell me, is the second bedroom large enough for an office?
Ben:	Yes, I think so.
Jeannie:	And are there two bathrooms?
Ben:	I'm afraid not.
Jeannie:	Hmm. Only one bathroom. That's a problem. Uh. Well, I'd like to see it anyway. Can we see the apartment this week?
Ben:	How about Friday afternoon?
Jeannie:	Friday afternoon? Uh . . . Friday afternoon? Yes, that's fine.
Ben:	What time is best?
Jeannie:	As late as possible.
Ben:	Let me see . . . how about 4:30?
Jeannie:	That's fine.
Ben:	All right then, I'll see you on Friday at 4:30. What is your name, please?
Jeannie:	Sure, it's Jeannie Campbell. C A M P B E L L.
Ben:	Okay, Mrs. Campbell. I'll expect you at 4:30 then.
Jeannie:	Oh. Before you hang up. What is the address?
Ben:	Oh. You're right. I didn't give it to you, did I? The address is 362 North Dover. That's D O V E R. It's a few blocks past the high school. You can't miss it.
Jeannie:	362 North Dover. Got it. Well, we'll see you on Friday. Good-bye.
Ben:	Good-bye.

Unit Thirteen

Interviewer: Yes, now, we're talking about training for your job.

Doctor: Well, it requires many years of study: four years at university, followed by, in my case, six years in medical school. But in the case of some, some people in the profession, uh, such as neurosurgeons, well, let's see, around ten years after college.

Interviewer: It sounds very tough to be in school until your late twenties or early thirties.

Doctor: It is, believe me. I don't think the average person understands what we go through. They think it's, uh, all glory.

Interviewer: Yes, well, what is your daily routine?

Doctor: Well, most of the day I spend at the office with the usual sorts of illnesses children get—colds, the flu, hmm—check-ups for school, that sort of thing.

Interviewer: But do you spend time at the hospital?

Doctor: Oh, yes. I do that first thing in the morning. I make my rounds at Mercy Hospital. That's where I send my patients. And sometimes I return in the afternoon, for example, if one of my patients has an operation in the morning.

Interviewer: And do you perform operations yourself?

Doctor: No, um, that's a surgeon's job. I . . . but I must be there in the case of children . . . um . . . to check on progress, cheer them up, talk to parents. You know.

Interviewer: Yes, I do.

Interviewer: And when did you begin this sort of work?

Tourist guide: Let's see now . . . um. Yes, six years ago this March.

Interviewer: And you enjoy it?

Tourist guide: Oh yes, very much. It is very tiring with long hours on the job, sometimes . . . uh . . . as much as 12 hours. Well uh, but it's exciting to meet people from all over the world. It really is.

Interviewer: What exactly do you do?

Tourist guide: Well, I take tourists to the famous places in the city, tell them the history of the places, talk about why they're famous. But, uh, then there's the other side.

Interviewer: What do you mean?

Tourist guide: Well, you know, when foreigners come to this country, things are very different. So, um, it is my job to give them advice, uh, help them with problems, and well, make them feel comfortable.

Interviewer:	And what special qualifications are necessary?
Tourist guide:	Well, uh, they have to enjoy meeting new people. And they, well, they must take special courses in the history of the city and things like that.
Interviewer:	And do they have to know foreign languages?
Tourist guide:	Yes, yes, that's a must. Otherwise, a tour company can use you only for the groups that speak English. And most of the tourists come from South America.
Interviewer:	South America. I see. So they speak Spanish?
Tourist guide:	That's right, Spanish. But my company will hire only people who speak at least two foreign languages.
Interviewer:	And you? How many languages do you speak?
Tourist guide:	Me? I speak three. Spanish, French, and Italian.
Interviewer:	Three languages? Then I can see why your work is so easy for you.

Unit Fourteen

Rosita:	Well, it's time for bed.
Charlie:	Bed? I think I'll stay up and watch a late movie or something. I'm not tired. You go to bed without me.
Rosita:	No, I'll stay up too. What's on?
Charlie:	Well, let's see. There's *Star Search*.
Rosita:	What's that?
Charlie:	A talent show.
Rosita:	No, I never like that kind of stuff.
Charlie:	Me neither. They're usually boring.
Rosita:	Besides, I'm not in the mood for music.
Charlie:	Well then, *Saturday Night Live* and *Wembley Music Festival* are out. They both have music. Let's see. There's *Benny Hill*.
Rosita:	That's that English guy, isn't it?
Charlie:	Yeah, I think so.
Rosita:	No, I don't want to watch that. I watched it once. I just didn't think anything was funny. Pretty stupid, if you ask me.
Charlie:	Then I guess it'll be a film. There's *The Amityville Horror*.
Rosita:	Are you in the mood for a horror film?
Charlie:	Not really. I'll get bad dreams from it. There's *The Santa Fe Trail* with Errol Flynn.
Rosita:	We saw that. Don't you remember? The one with Ronald Reagan? What else is on?
Charlie:	Uh. *The Man Who Would Be King* and *The Reincarnation of Peter Proud*.
Rosita:	*The Reincarnation of Peter Proud*. Isn't that with Jennifer O'Neill?

Charlie: Uh, yeah.

Rosita: Andy saw that. She said it was terrible. One of the worst films ever. Don't you remember?

Charlie: No, I don't. But your sister, she says all the films are terrible. But anyway, that leaves us with *The Man Who Would Be King.* Actually, it sounds pretty good. Sean Connery and Michael Caine.

Rosita: Good. Let's watch that. I just love Sean Connery and ... uh ... Michael Caine, he isn't so bad either.

Charlie: Okay. Channel 33 it is then.

Unit Fifteen

Jimmy: What time?

Karen: Around 2:00 is fine.

Jimmy: Now I know that I take the number 5 bus and get off at the Art Cinema. But where is your place from there?

Karen: It's not far. When you get off the bus at the Art Cinema, turn left and walk along City Line Avenue. You'll see Mama's Italian Restaurant on your right.

Jimmy: Mama's on the right.

Karen: The first street on the left is called Berk. Make a left there.

Jimmy: Left at Berk.

Karen: Berk is only one block long. So turn again at State Street. There you'll make a left.

Jimmy: Left on State.

Karen: So, it's left on Berk and left on State. Now walk down State until you come to Jefferson Avenue. Then turn right.

Jimmy: Right on Jefferson.

Karen: Walk three blocks down Jefferson. When you pass the elementary school, make a right.

Jimmy: What's the name of the street?

Karen: That's Bell. It's my street.

Jimmy: So, I make a left on Bell.

Karen: No, you make a right.

Jimmy: Sorry. Right.

Karen: My house is across the street from the Pagoda Chinese Restaurant. It's right after you cross Oak Street, at the end of Bell Street.

Jimmy: Is your house the first one on the block?

Karen: No, it's the third after Oak.

Jimmy: Third house after Oak.

Karen: Right. 5310.

Jimmy: Okay. Let's see now. Left from the bus, left at Berk, left at State, right at Jefferson and right at Bell, third house after Oak, across the street from the Chinese restaurant.

Karen: You've got it.

Jimmy: Okay. See you around 2:00. Bye.

Karen: Bye.

Unit Sixteen

Waitress: Good afternoon. Are you ready to order?

Juan: Yes, I think so. Betty, what will you have?

Betty: I think I'll start off with a cup of soup. What kind of soup do you
            have today?

Waitress: Clam chowder and chicken rice.

Betty: I'll have a cup of chicken rice.

Waitress: Yes.

Betty: And a hamburger with french fries.

Waitress: Deluxe or regular?

Betty: I think the regular will be fine.

Waitress: Anything to drink?

Betty: Uh, yes, iced tea.

Waitress: And you, sir?

Juan: Uh, ah yes, can you tell me what a pizza burger is?

Waitress: That's a hamburger covered with tomato sauce and mozzarella
            cheese.

Juan: No, I don't think so. That's not for me. How about a cold salad
            platter? What does the tuna fish salad platter come with?

Waitress: Lettuce, tomato, hard-boiled egg, cole slaw, and potato salad.

Juan: That sounds good. I'll have that.

Waitress: One tuna fish salad platter.

Juan: And a cup of coffee, please.

Waitress: A cup of coffee. Would you like any dessert? Ice cream? Chocolate
            cake? Apple pie?

Juan: No, thanks. Not for me.

Waitress: And you ma'am?

Betty: Uh, no. I don't think so.

Waitress: So that's a cup of soup, a hamburger and fries, a tuna fish salad
            platter, an iced tea, and a cup of coffee. Fine, thanks.

Betty: Oh yes, excuse me.

Waitress: Yes?

Betty: Yes. Can we have some water, too?

Waitress: I'll get you some right away.

Betty: Thanks.

Unit Seventeen

Yazid: Excuse me.

Secretary: Yes, can I help you?

Yazid: Yes, uh . . . I want to take an English course in September, and I need some information.

Secretary: Sure. Courses start on September 6th and finish right before Christmas on December 22nd. Um . . . the advanced classes meet every Monday, Wednesday, and Friday, from 6 to 8 in the evening. Registration is one week before classes begin. So that's August 30th.

Yazid: So, there are no classes on Tuesday and Thursday?

Secretary: No, not for advanced students. Only Monday, Wednesday, and Friday.

Yazid: And the registration date is August the 30th?

Secretary: Yes, that's right.

Yazid: And how much is the tuition for the one course from September 6th to December 22nd?

Secretary: It's 350 dollars. And if you want to continue in January, that will be another 350.

Yazid: 350 dollars. Hmm. Could you tell me what's in the advanced courses?

Secretary: Let me see. There's advanced grammar, American literature, and conversation.

Yazid: Is there any work on pronunciation?

Secretary: No, not at this level.

Yazid: How about writing? Is there anything on composition?

Secretary: Yes, they do some writing, but most of the work is on grammar, literature, and conversation.

Yazid: So, there's grammar, literature, conversation, and some writing. I see. And just a few more questions. Do you have a language lab where I can work on my pronunciation? And what about videos and computers?

Secretary: Well, we don't have a language lab. The building's too small. But we do have video and we also have tape recorders in every room.

Yazid: And computers?

Secretary: No, none at present.

Yazid: I see. Well, thank you very much. You're very helpful.

Secretary: You're welcome. Good-bye.

Yazid: Good-bye.

Unit Eighteen

Eileen: First of all, you need a square piece of paper. No, not that one. That's rectangular. It has to be square, or you won't be able to make it right.

Martha: All right. This is square.

Eileen: Now I want you to fold. Let's see, I want you to fold each corner of the paper into the middle of the paper.

Martha: Like this?

Eileen: Yeah. And fold them down. Each piece should be the same size. Okay. And turn the paper over.

Martha: Uh-huh.

Eileen: Okay. And fold each corner again to the middle.

Martha: Okay.

Eileen: Now fold the paper over in the middle.

Martha: Yeah.

Eileen: Fold it so you have a line. Okay. Now open it up again and fold it the other way so you have another line. Right.

Martha: Okay.

Eileen: Okay. Now, you have two sides of paper. On one side of paper, um, you have, um, what looks like triangles and on the other side you have what looks like little squares, little boxes.

Martha: Huh.

Eileen: On each square write one name you like. A different name on each square.

Martha: Any square?

Eileen: Any square. Turn the paper over so you're looking at the four triangles. Right. Now, on each big triangle are two small triangles.

Martha: These?

Eileen: Yeah. On four small triangles write four numbers, any numbers but small ones.

Martha: On the four small triangles?

Eileen: Yeah, but on two big triangles that are opposite each other, not next to each other.

Martha: Like this?

Eileen: Uh-huh. Okay. Now, on the other four small triangles write four colors.

Martha: Finished.

Eileen: Okay. Now you have four numbers and four colors. Lift up the triangles. On the back, uh-uh, on the back of the triangles write eight things about the future, eight things about my future.

Martha: Good or bad?

Eileen: Whatever you want, but things like, "You will have eight babies."

Martha: Where?

Eileen:	One prediction on the other side of a number.
Martha:	For all the numbers?
Eileen:	And all the colors. But let me show you how mine works first.
Martha:	Okay.
Eileen:	I put my thumb and second finger under two boxes.
Martha:	Like this.
Eileen:	And the other thumb and other second finger under the other two boxes so I can move the fortune teller like this.
Martha:	Yeah.
Eileen:	Now, what name do you like?
Martha:	Steven.
Eileen:	So I spell the name and move my fingers with each letter. S T E V E N. Now, what number do you like?
Martha:	Six.
Eileen:	S I X. What color do you like?
Martha:	Blue.
Eileen:	Blue. You will get married six times.
Martha:	Ha, ha.

ROUND THREE
Unit Nineteen

Announcer:	And now, ladies and gentlemen, it's time for The Fame Game. And here he is, your host, Art Newhope.
Art Newhope:	Hello, everybody. Welcome to The Fame Game, where you and our contestants here in the studio try to guess the names of famous people. Let's welcome tonight's contestants. Here is Mark Stewart all the way from Oklahoma City. How are you tonight, Mark?
Mark Stewart:	Just fine, Art.
Art:	That's good. And from Portland, Oregon, Sheila Stevenson. Welcome, Sheila.
Sheila Stevenson:	Thank you, Art.
Art:	Now, before we begin, let me explain the rules of the game. I will give you some clues about a famous person. Many people don't know this information about our famous person, but it's all true. If you can guess who this person is with only this information, then you get one thousand dollars and ten points. If not, then you can ask me questions, five questions from each of you. But remember, I can answer only with a yes or a no. The person who guesses the name first gets the ten points.

	Are you ready?
Sheila:	Yes, Art.
Mark:	Yes, Art.
Art:	Right. Then, here we go. My father was the first prime minister of my country. I went to university in England. I had two sons, and I met with many world leaders during my lifetime. And there you have it, Sheila and Mark, a mini-picture of our first famous person. For one thousand dollars, what is the name of this famous person? Okay. Question time. First you, Mark.
Mark:	Let's see. You said your father was a prime minister. That means you weren't American. Were you from Europe?
Art:	No, I wasn't. Sheila?
Sheila:	Were you born in the 20th century?
Art:	Yes, I was. Mark?
Mark:	Yes. You weren't from Europe. Were you from South America?
Art:	No, I wasn't. Sheila?
Sheila:	Right. You weren't from South America. Were you from Asia?
Art:	Yes, I was. Mark?
Mark:	Asian, born in the 20th century. Were you an actor or actress?
Art:	No, I wasn't. Sheila?
Sheila:	Were you a writer?
Art:	No, I wasn't. Mark?
Mark:	How about politics? Were you a politician?
Art:	Yes, I was. Sheila?
Sheila:	An Asian politician. Let's see. Did you die in the 1980s?
Art:	Yes, I did. Mark, your last question?
Mark:	You said your father was a prime minister. Were you a prime minister, too?
Art:	Yes, I was. And now, Sheila, the final question of this round.
Sheila:	Were you killed by gunmen?
Art:	Yes, I was. And there you have it. Now, take 15 seconds to write down your answers. And you in the audience write down the name of this famous person too.

And now for your answer. Sheila, can we see your card? That's right, Indira Gandhi. And your card, Mark? Indira Gandhi. So you both have ten points. Now, let's go on to our second famous person and see if we can break the tie.

Unit Twenty

Doctor:	Ms. Santini, would you come in, please? Have a seat. I want to ask you a few questions before I examine you.
Michele Santini:	Certainly.
Doctor:	First of all, how old are you?
Michele:	27.
Doctor:	And your height, how tall are you?
Michele:	I think I'm 5 feet 6.
Doctor:	5 feet 6 inches. Well, we'll check to make sure. And how much do you weigh?
Michele:	Around 145 pounds.
Doctor:	145. Uh-huh. Do you smoke?
Michele:	No, never.
Doctor:	How about alcoholic beverages? Do you drink much wine or beer?
Michele:	Very rarely. If I go out to dinner, I sometimes have a glass of wine.
Doctor:	Uh-huh. And do you exercise regularly?
Michele:	Only in the summer when I have time to swim.
Doctor:	So you don't do any exercise for say, oh, 9 months out of the year.
Michele:	No. I never seem to find the time.
Doctor:	All right. Now. About your recent medical history. In the past few months did you have any colds?
Michele:	No. Uh. No, I don't think so.
Doctor:	Any sore throats?
Michele:	No.
Doctor:	Any bad coughs?
Michele:	No.
Doctor:	And the flu?
Michele:	No, not in years.
Doctor:	What about stomachaches?
Michele:	Uh. Uh. Yeah. Last month I had a bad stomachache from some fish I ate. I was in bed the whole day. I even missed work.
Doctor:	But no stomach problems since then?
Michele:	No.
Doctor:	How about headaches?
Michele:	Oh, I get a headache every once in a while. In fact, I had a terrible one last night, but I took a couple of aspirins and it went away.
Doctor:	I see. And do you ever get earaches?
Michele:	No, never.

Doctor:	How about your teeth? Do you have any serious problems?
Michele:	Well, last month I had a slight toothache, but I went to the dentist and she took care of it.
Doctor:	Now, just a few more questions. Do you ever get muscle pains?
Michele:	Only backaches. I occasionally get bad pains in my lower back.
Doctor:	Maybe more exercise will help.
Michele:	I know.
Doctor:	No pains in your chest?
Michele:	No.
Doctor:	Arms?
Michele:	No.
Doctor:	Legs?
Michele:	No.
Doctor:	Have you ever broken your leg?
Michele:	No.
Doctor:	Sprained your ankle?
Michele:	No, not that I can remember.
Doctor:	And have you ever broken your arm?
Michele:	Once when I was 12. I fell off my bike and broke my arm and two fingers.
Doctor:	Okay, Ms. Santini, if you'll roll up your sleeve, I'll take your blood pressure.

Unit Twenty-One

Jackson:	Hello. General Repair. Milt Jackson speaking. Can I help you?
Henderson:	Hello. Do you fix washing machines?
Jackson:	No, we don't.
Henderson:	Okay. Thank you.
ABC:	Good morning. ABC Appliances.
Henderson:	Hello. Do you fix washing machines?
ABC:	Yes, we do.
Henderson:	How much do you charge?
ABC:	$50 an hour. Of course parts are additional.
Henderson:	Did you say 50 or 15?
ABC:	50.
Henderson:	Can you come by and look at my machine today?
ABC:	I'm afraid today is impossible and tomorrow too. What about the day after tomorrow? Wednesday afternoon.
Henderson:	Wednesday. Hmm. Okay, let me think about it. I'll call you back.
ABC:	That's fine. Good-bye.

C & R:	Hello.
Henderson:	Hello. Is this C & R Repair?
C & R:	Yes, it is.
Henderson:	Do you fix washing machines?
C & R:	What kind do you have?
Henderson:	A General Electric.
C & R:	Yes, we repair General Electrics. We charge $40 an hour, and any parts are additional.
Henderson:	You said 40?
C & R:	Yes, that's right.
Henderson:	How long will it take to repair the machine?
C & R:	I don't know because I don't know the problem.
Henderson:	I see. Well, when can you come?
C & R:	Tomorrow afternoon.
Henderson:	No sooner?
C & R:	No, I'm afraid not.
Henderson:	Well, O.K. What time will your repairman come?
C & R:	How about 2 o'clock?
Henderson:	That's fine.
C & R:	Can I have your name and address, please?
Henderson:	Joan Henderson, 2803 Market Street.
C & R:	2803 Market. All right. Our repairman will be at your place at 2 tomorrow.
Henderson:	What is the name of the repairman, please? I like to know the names of strangers before I let them in my house.
C & R:	I understand. Let me see. Yes. Your repairman will be John Miller, M I L L E R.
Henderson:	John Miller. Thank you. I'll expect him at 2 tomorrow.
C & R:	Fine. Good-bye.
Henderson:	Good-bye.

Unit Twenty-Two

Al Martinez:	Come in.
Eleanor Lance:	Hello. I'm Eleanor Lance.
Al:	Yes. Please, come in. Sit down. I'm Al Martinez, uh, owner and manager of the Grande Dining Restaurant. You're interested in a job here?
Eleanor:	Yes, I am. I saw your ad in this morning's paper, and I decided to come and apply immediately.
Al:	Yes. Good. Well, tell me, Miss, uh, Miss . . .
Eleanor:	Lance, Eleanor Lance.
Al:	Yes. Sorry, Miss Lance. Tell me now, do you have any experience in the restaurant business?

Eleanor:	Yes, a lot. I worked, uh, as a waitress for about 3 years at the Marriott Inn, and I also worked at the Olympia Diner at the same time for about, uh, let's see, about 9 months, yes. I was a cashier there.
Al:	Uh-huh. I see. Well, what position are you applying for here?
Eleanor:	Well, I want a waitress job, but I can also work as a cashier.
Al:	Yes. Well, we *are* looking for waitresses, and you seem to have a lot of experience. We want waitresses with a lot of experience. Now, what about hours? Are you interested in full-time work or part-time work?
Eleanor:	Well, I'm really interested in full time.
Al:	I see. Well, we like to start our waitresses part time first and give them more hours slowly. However, you seem to have a lot of experience. Hmm. Well, let's see what we can do. Now we serve lunch and dinner, no breakfast. Can you work in the evenings?
Eleanor:	Yes, I can. I can do both day and evening work, but I'd prefer evening work.
Al:	Good. Okay then. Let's start with dinner four nights a week, and, uh, we'll go from there. Oh, by the way, Miss Lance, how will you be coming to work? By car? By bus?
Eleanor:	Well, I don't have a car. I'll be coming by bus.
Al:	Oh, I see. That'll be a problem if we, uh, if we need you right away.
Eleanor:	I'll get here as soon as I can.
Al:	Well, that's a problem. Well, we'll see. Okay Miss Lance. We'll be in touch. Oh, and when could you start?
Eleanor:	Oh, right away.
Al:	That's good. Okay then, Miss Lance. I'll call you tomorrow and let you know. Thank you for coming.
Eleanor:	Thank you. Good-bye.
Al:	Good-bye.
Al:	Come in.
Lisa:	Hello. Are you Mr. Martinez?
Al:	Yes, I am. Please come in.
Lisa:	Thank you.
Al:	Sit down, please. You're Miss?
Lisa:	Alder, Lisa Alder. I'm Bob Alder's daughter. He owns the supermarket just down the street.
Al:	Oh yes. Of course I know him. We used to work together at a store years ago. How *is* your father?
Lisa:	Oh, he's fine, thank you.

Al:	That's good. Well, did he tell you we're looking for waitresses?
Lisa:	Well, no. I read your ad in the paper, so I came over to apply.
Al:	Well, that's good. What experience have you had?
Lisa:	Well, uh, I worked at Tom's Restaurant, the one on Broadway, for about 8 months, and then, well, I worked at my father's supermarket.
Al:	Yes. But have you had any other waitressing experience?
Lisa:	Well, no, but I learn very fast, and I was pretty good at Tom's Restaurant. They will give me a good reference.
Al:	I see. Well, are you interested in full-time or part-time work?
Lisa:	Well, I'm thinking about part time, actually. A few hours a day. Maybe lunchtime.
Al:	Well, we do serve lunch and dinner, maybe lunch to start, one or two days a week. Well. Can you work evenings?
Lisa:	Hmm. Not really, well, I go to school in the evenings and I also have to study. Working lunchtime really fits into my schedule, Mr. Martinez.
Al:	Well, Miss Alder, we'll see what we can do. Oh, by the way, how will you come to work?
Lisa;	Well, I live within walking distance, just two blocks away.
Al:	Good. Then you can walk over with no problem if we call you at the last minute. That's good. Can you start right away?
Lisa:	Oh yes.
Al:	I'll be in touch then.
Lisa:	Thanks very much, Mr. Martinez.
Al:	Say hello to your father for me.
Lisa:	I will. Good-bye.
Al:	Good-bye.

Unit Twenty-Three

Good afternoon, everybody. This is Ronald Jaffe with this week's edition of Movie Talk. First, let's look at the films this week in area theaters: *The Kid Rides Again, When You Find Love,* and *Wronged.*

The last of the three, *Wronged,* is definitely the best, in fact, one of the best films in a long time, with Henry Michaelson and Joanne Seymour. It is about a man who gets a life sentence for a murder he did not commit. In the style of the films of the 40s and 50s, it is a modern story of a man and his wife, wonderfully played by Joanne Seymour. They fight to make people believe Thompson is the wrong man and not the killer. The strength of their love is wonderful even after Thompson has been in prison for 15 years. Of course, I won't tell you what happens after Thompson's 15th year in prison. That would ruin the story. But if you see no other film, you should see this one. The story may be old, but the acting is great and it will hold your attention from beginning to end.

Unfortunately, I can't say the same for *When You Find Love*. Just another silly story about boy meets girl, boy loses girl, boy gets girl again, and they live happily ever after. Will Hollywood ever get tired of such stupid films? Set on a New England college campus, the star of the movie, Tommy Seal, is a freshman. He meets the older, two years older, Stephanie Fall, played by Sally Evans. In real life she must be at least 30, not 20. Well, Billy, our hero, has a hard time with Stephanie. After all, he is so much younger. But they fall in love, in about a minute, as long as it takes to take a picture with a Polaroid. And they are both so happy, in true paradise, until, that is, until Buck, the star football player, played by Ronco Star, the only good acting in the film, steals Stephanie away from poor Billy. He is, after all, a senior and football star. And the rest of the film is about, naturally, how Billy gets Stephanie back, making her remember their love. He shows her that he and not Buck is the man for her. Well, if you can stand a stupid story and bad acting, then take your 8-year-old child to see *When You Find Love*. Anyone older will leave the theater before the movie ends.

And finally, *The Kid Rides Again*, a western about a young cowboy, Kit Barnes, who stops the bad guys, the robbers, killers, and plain old bullies, and helps the good guys. Kit is fast with a gun, and never once in this cowboy story does he ever get a scratch on himself. In the style of the old-fashioned cowboy, Kit is the cowboy who never stays in one place for a very long time, who leads a lonely but very free life. Nothing new on the story line but a good classic-style western with good acting. Peter Sells as Kit catches just the right mood. He's an excellent and natural cowboy. There are beautiful scenes of the open country in the west and enough action to hold your interest. A good cowboy film for those who, like me, always enjoy seeing the old west. And now, before we go on to news from Hollywood, a word from our sponsor.

Unit Twenty-Four

Policewoman:	Now, sir, can you tell me exactly what happened?
Witness:	Yes, I think so. I was right here watching three, three?, yes three children playing ball in front of the school. It's a dangerous place for children to be playing. I wonder where their parents are. Really! Some people!
Policewoman:	Yes, sir, go on.
Witness:	Anyway, a white Volkswagen came up on the right-hand side of the street.
Policewoman:	Did you say a white Volkswagen?

Witness:	Uh-huh. There was a bus in front of it, but the bus turned left at the corner. And at the same time a truck came down the other side of the street. What make was it? Uh. Let me think.
Policewoman:	It's not important. Just go on.
Witness:	Well, the Volkswagen stopped at the red traffic light and then went on. Well, just at that moment, one of the children kicked the ball into the street and a little boy ran after it.
Policewoman:	So a boy ran into the street.
Witness:	He sure did and right in front of the truck too. The driver of the truck slammed on the brakes but he had to turn to the left. That's how he ran into the bus. Uh. Okay. There was a woman sitting near the bus stop. She saw the whole thing too. Why don't you ask her? She'll tell you the exact same thing.
Policewoman:	Don't worry, sir. We'll talk to everyone, but which driver was to blame?
Witness:	Why, neither driver! It was the child's fault, clear and simple, coming out between two parked cars. I don't understand how parents can let their children play in such dangerous places. Really! Parents today! They should . . .
Policewoman:	Thank you, sir. You are very helpful. If we have any other questions, we'll be in touch.
Witness:	You're welcome, officer. But those parents should be put in jail. When I was . . .

Unit Twenty-Five

Ladies and gentlemen, before we get to the hotel, I'd like to go over the program for tomorrow. If you will take a look at page 2 of your itinerary, please.

Okay. The bus will pick you up at 8:15 tomorrow morning. Please be outside the hotel by then. We have a busy day tomorrow and we want to do everything. Please go down for breakfast between 7 and 7:30 so you have plenty of time. So 8:15 then. Okay? Our first stop will be the White House, the home of every American president since 1800. It doesn't open until 10, but we'll have to get there before that. We'll have to wait in line. I'm afraid everyone has to. There are 132 rooms in the White House. We can't see all of them, but we will see the famous Green Room, Blue Room, and Red Room and also the beautiful Rose Garden. If we're lucky, we may get a glimpse of the President or a member of the family, but naturally we will not visit their living quarters. After all, they need their privacy too.

Okay. We'll leave the White House a little before 12 o'clock so you can have an hour for lunch. The bus will take you to an area with several restaurants. Maybe you'll even see someone famous. But remember, you only have one hour for lunch, from 12 to 1 o'clock. The bus will depart at 1 o'clock sharp for the

Smithsonian Institution. The Smithsonian is made up of seven museums. Naturally, we won't visit all of them. We'll visit the National Air and Space Museum. This museum opened in 1976. In it we'll see Charles Lindbergh's Spirit of St. Louis and Gemini IV. How many of you remember that? The first walk in outer space took place from it back in 1965. And we'll also see a piece of moon rock.

From the Smithsonian we'll head for the Washington Monument. This was built in honor of George Washington, and it opened to the public in 1888. It stands 555 feet and 5 inches high. It is the tallest building in Washington. I'm afraid you won't have time to climb the 897 steps to the top. You will have time to go up by elevator. The view is spectacular.

Before crossing the Potomac for Arlington Cemetery, our last stop of the day, we'll visit the Lincoln Memorial, which was built in honor of Abraham Lincoln in 1922. The 19-foot statue of Lincoln is one of the most impressive in Washington. We'll then take a ride across the Potomac River to Arlington Cemetery. There we'll see the Tomb of the Unknown Soldier. Sixty thousand soldiers and other great Americans are buried at Arlington. Our last stop will be at the graves of President John F. Kennedy and Senator Robert Kennedy. We will be back at the hotel between 6 and 7. You'll have plenty of time to relax over dinner, but try to make it an early night. We'll have a long day on Friday when we visit Capitol Hill and Independence Hall and the Liberty Bell in Philadelphia. But more about that tomorrow. Well, here we are at the hotel. Enjoy your first night in Washington. Are there any questions? Yes?

Unit Twenty-Six

Well, as you've seen, drowning results in death because air doesn't get into the lungs. This causes death because the body needs oxygen. Oxygen is carried to all parts of the body by the blood. Uh. The heart pumps blood to all parts of the body, and we're going to be studying the heart. But before we look at it in detail, I'd like to give you a general overview.

The heart is a muscle like a machine. This machine pumps blood to all parts of the body. So if the heart stops and no longer pumps the blood, the person doesn't get the oxygen he or she needs. And that's why the person dies. The heart muscle . . . the heart is the only muscle that must continuously work.

Your heart is about the size of your fist. So make a fist and you can see the size of your heart. A man's heart weighs about 11 ounces and a woman's around 9 ounces. An adult heart is about 5 inches long, 3-1/2 inches wide, and 2-1/2 inches thick. The normal heart beats about 70 times a minute and more than 100,000 times in a single day. Ten pints of blood go through the heart every 60 seconds.

The heart lies near the middle of the chest, between the lungs. It's wider at the top than it is at the bottom, and the wider end, the top, points toward the right shoulder. The narrower end, the bottom, points toward the left. It's the lower end you can feel beating. Try to feel the heart beating. But the heart is not on the left side of the body. As I said before, it's near the middle of your chest.

The heart is divided into the left and the right side and the top and the bottom. On the top, at the top part of the heart are the two atria and on the bottom part of the heart are the two ventricles. The atria are smaller than the ventricles. The atria at the top collect blood coming to the heart from the veins. On the bottom, the ventricles, the largest part of the heart, pump blood into the arteries. Then the arteries take the blood to the rest of the body. So the veins bring the blood to the heart and the arteries carry the blood to the other parts of the body.

As I mentioned before, the heart is divided into the left side and the right side. The blood entering the right side contains carbon dioxide. This is a waste product we have to breathe out when we breathe in air with oxygen. When the blood enters the right side of the heart with the carbon dioxide, it goes first into the right atrium, then into the right ventricle. Next, to the lungs so the carbon dioxide can be removed there in the lungs. Then fresh air, and fresh oxygen rather, can enter the blood.

From the lungs the blood goes back to the heart—to the left side of the heart. First, the blood goes from the lungs to the left atrium and then to the left ventricle. The blood is then pumped to the rest of the body. It leaves the left ventricle, which pumps the blood through the aorta so it can go to the other parts of the body. Uh. Let me repeat that last stage for you. From the lungs, the blood with fresh oxygen goes to the left atria, then the left ventricle, and then into the aorta where the blood leaves for all parts of the body. And that is a simplified description of how the heart works. We'll look at it, we'll look at it in more detail in our next session. Are there any questions?

Unit Twenty-Seven

For tomorrow the forecast is good with clear and sunny skies and temperatures in the mid-70s. And finally here is a human interest story. The police are looking into a report by two truck drivers. They saw strange creatures on Route 65 two days ago. The two drivers, Don Anderson and William Elkins, both 32 years old from Chicago, saw three strange creatures as they were eating at a picnic site on Route 65 between York and Hilltown at 3 o'clock on Sunday. According to them, the creatures were about 3 feet tall with four eyes and no mouths. Their ears were the same size as their heads. They looked exactly like one another and communicated by making strange noises. The truck drivers said this sounded like some sort of music.

As soon as the creatures saw the truck drivers, they ran behind the trees. The two men were also frightened. When they got a good look at these unusual beings, they ran right back to their truck and drove off, leaving their sandwiches and beer behind. Maybe they should drink orange juice instead of beer! And that's it for the 6 o'clock evening news. Join us at 11 o'clock for more news and visions of E.T. in our own backyard.